THE ART OF WOODWORKING

CLASSIC AMERICAN FURNITURE

THE ART OF WOODWORKING

CLASSIC AMERICAN FURNITURE

TIME-LIFE BOOKS
ALEXANDRIA, VIRGINIA

ST. REMY PRESS
MONTREAL

THE ART OF WOODWORKING was produced by
ST. REMY PRESS

Publisher	Kenneth Winchester
President/Chief Executive Officer	Fernand Lecoq
President/Chief Operating Officer	Pierre Léveillé
Series Editor	Pierre Home-Douglas
Series Art Director	Francine Lemieux
Senior Editor	Marc Cassini
Editor	Andrew Jones
Art Directors	Jean-Pierre Bourgeois, Michel Giguère
Designers	François Daxhelet, Jean-Guy Doiron
	François Longpré
Picture Editor	Christopher Jackson
Writers	John Dowling, Adam Van Sertima
Contributing Illustrators	Gilles Beauchemin, Michel Blais,
	Ronald Durepos, Michael Stockdale,
	James Thérien
Administrator	Natalie Watanabe
Production Manager	Michelle Turbide
Coordinator	Dominique Gagné
System Coordinator	Eric Beaulieu
Photographer	Robert Chartier
Indexer	Christine M. Jacobs

Time-Life Books is a division of Time Life Inc.,
a wholly owned subsidiary of
THE TIME INC. BOOK COMPANY

TIME-LIFE INC.

President and CEO	John M. Fahey

TIME-LIFE BOOKS

President	John D. Hall
Managing Editor	Roberta Conlan
Director of Design	Michael Hentges
Director of Editorial Operations	Ellen Robling
Consulting Editor	John R. Sullivan
Vice-President, Book Production	Marjann Caldwell
Production Manager	Marlene Zack
Quality Assurance Manager	James King

THE CONSULTANTS

Jon Arno is a consultant, cabinetmaker, and freelance writer who lives in Troy, Michigan. He conducts seminars on wood identification and early American furniture design, and is the author of *The Woodworkers Visual Handbook*, published by Rodale Press.

Mike Dunbar builds fine furniture at his workshop in Portsmouth, New Hampshire and offers Windsor chair making seminars across North America. He is a contributing editor of *American Woodworker* and author of *Federal Furniture* and *Make A Windsor Chair With Michael Dunbar*, both published by The Taunton Press.

Giles Miller-Mead taught advanced cabinetmaking at Montreal technical schools for more than 10 years. A native of New Zealand, he has worked as a restorer of antique furniture.

Classic American furniture.
 p. cm. — (The Art of woodworking)
Includes index.
ISBN 0-8094-9542-2
1. Furniture making. I. Time-Life Books. II. Series.
TT194.C53 1995
749.213—dc20   95-21990
                                            CIP

For information about any Time-Life book,
please call 1-800-621-7026, or write:
Reader Information
Time-Life Customer Service
P.O. Box C-32068
Richmond, Virginia
23261-2068

R 10 9 8 7 6 5 4 3 2 1

CONTENTS

Dr. John Kassay on
WINDSOR FURNITURE

A deceptively well-engineered furniture style whose parts are assembled mainly from wooden sticks, Windsor represents one of history's most innovative and recognizable furniture designs. The Windsor family of furniture consists of stools, chairs, cradles, stands, and tables. Chairs are the largest category with eight different basic forms, such as comb-backs, step-downs, and the sack-back version, which is featured beginning on page 70. Chairs also spawned nine derivatives that include stools, rocking chairs, writing armchairs, and child-sized chairs.

The origin of Windsors is ancient history. Their antecedents can be attributed to the Egyptians, where tomb drawings of the 18th Dynasty depict workmen sitting on three-legged hand-hewn stools socketed to a plank seat. The reason for the name Windsor is something of an enigma, but the most logical explanation is that they were named during the first decade of the 18th Century after the English town of Windsor, whose beech trees provided a plentiful supply of raw material for legs and other turned parts.

Windsor chairs improved on the traditional joiner's chairs of the period by eliminating the need to glue-up seat frames. In a Windsor chair, the seat is a solid plank serving as the foundation for the legs and stretchers and for the spindle back. That simplicity and strength of design is no doubt one of the keys to the chair's undying popularity and longevity.

Windsor chair making started as a cottage industry in England during the 1720s, but soon became an important factory-based operation, employing hundreds of workers, centered in the town of High Wycombe. Although the first Windsors in America were chairs imported from England, Philadelphia chair makers almost immediately capitalized on this popular new form of easily made seating. Their one-man shops expanded into large factories.

English chair makers took advantage of the physical properties of different woods for different components of the chairs, using ash for bent parts, beech for turnings, and elm for seats. Their American counterparts used hickory, red oak or ash for bending, maple for turnings, and pine for seats. Windsors were traditionally painted green, but other colors such as blue, mustard and red were also used. The paint concealed the different wood colors and served to protect the wood outdoors, while conveying a unifying wholeness to the piece. Many English chairs were simply dip stained.

Now retired, Dr. John Kassay taught furniture design for 30 years at San Francisco State University. His Book of Shaker Furniture, *published by the University of Massachussetts Press, is considered one of the foremost reference books on Shaker style. He is currently preparing a similar book on Windsor furniture for the same publisher. He lives in San Bruno, California.*

Gregory Weidman talks about the
APPEAL OF FEDERAL STYLE

As a graduate student at the Winterthur Museum Program in Early American Culture, I was privileged to work with the country's premiere collection of American furniture, including the best examples of the styles most popular with cabinetmakers today—Queen Anne and Chippendale. Even in this setting, though, I was always drawn to the neoclassical pieces of the later Federal and Empire eras. As curator of the Maryland Historical Society in Baltimore 17 years later, I am still studying and writing about those wonderful pieces that I found so appealing.

The Federal era in America began with independence from England. This political change also ushered in a new period in the arts. The Federal style represented an esthetic revolution over the popular Chippendale and Rococo styles. The prominent features of the earlier periods—florid, naturalistic carving, asymmetry in ornament, and architectural massiveness in case furniture—were all derived from a hodgepodge of historical and contemporary sources. Federal furniture replaced these artistic excesses with a clean, linear style that looked back to just one source of inspiration—Ancient Classicism.

The great neoclassical architect/interior designer Robert Adam introduced the new style to the English gentry, and furniture designers George Hepplewhite and Thomas Sheraton published highly influential books that popularized its ancient Greek and Roman decorative motifs.

In the United States, this new style—sometimes also referred to as "Hepplewhite" or "Sheraton"—was the height of fashion by the mid-1790s. Although each metropolitan area developed its own distinctive form of Federal style, there were certain basic characteristics that defined it. The pieces in general are light and delicate, with attenuated elements such as tapered legs. Surface are flat and linear, relying on geometric patterns of veneer and banding in contrasting woods to achieve the main esthetic effects. Ornamentation is primarily inlaid and patterned stringing and pictorial motifs. Decorative elements are derived from ancient classical sources: columns, shells, urns, swags, leaves and vines, with one distinctively American motif: the patriotic eagle, symbol of the new nation.

By about 1810, Federal style began to evolve into Late Neoclassical or Empire taste, which was even more closely inspired by archaeological discoveries. Actual pieces of ancient furniture such as "klismos" chairs, banqueting couches, and tripod stands were reproduced by cabinetmakers. Not until the 1840s and the advent of romantic Victorian revival styles was the taste for the Classical superseded in the American home.

Gregory Weidman is Curator of the Maryland Historical Society in Baltimore, home of America's largest collection of Federal furniture.

Norm Vandal explains
QUEEN ANNE'S LINE OF BEAUTY

I n material objects such as furniture, I believe beauty is born from pleasing proportion and the harmonious relationship between curved and straight lines. Straight lines impart structure, mass, and solidity. Curved lines lend movement, elegance, and grace. To me, Queen Anne-style furniture presents the perfect union of straight and curved components. Simple lines, graceful curves, unpretentious decoration, and delicate proportion all contribute to some of the most beautiful expressions in American furniture.

Queen Anne is a name given to a style of furniture first produced in the American Colonies in the early to mid 18th Century. Assigning periods or historical epochs to furniture styles, however, is solely useful for discussions about their origins. This style saw only embryonic development during the reign of Queen Anne herself, yet it remains immensely popular to this day. Indeed, while I am certainly not an 18th Century cabinetmaker, most of the pieces I've produced in my rural, one-man shop have been in this elegant style, and they have ranged from faithful reproductions of period pieces to modern adaptations.

What are the hallmarks of Queen Anne furniture? The most prominent feature is the cabriole leg, a sculptured, three-dimensional form based on animal motifs. Other essential characteristics include the scrolled aprons of tables, chairs and case pieces; the vase-shaped splats of chair backs; the scrolled pediments of high chests and secretaries; the arch-panel doors of secretaries and cupboards; and the shell carvings on chair crests, dressing tables, and other case pieces. Virtually all of these elements are dependent on the curve, on the S-shaped so-called "line of beauty."

In becoming familiar with any style of furniture, you eventually recognize how style is evolutionary, how it develops and changes with the accretion of new ideas. All design is in constant flux at any of its stages. I take great pleasure in examining furniture for vestiges of the Queen Anne style, both in period pieces and in new designs from the shops of contemporary craftsmen. I don't ask "Is this piece Queen Anne?" but rather "What are the Queen Anne characteristics of this particular piece, and do any other elements contribute to or conflict with the effective beauty of its design?" In this way, the old is constantly blended with the new—a stockpot in the kitchen of ideas.

Norm Vandal builds reproduction furniture in his Roxbury, Vermont shop and teaches literature at a nearby high school. He is the author of Queen Anne Furniture, *published by The Taunton Press.*

CLASSIC AMERICAN FURNITURE STYLES

QUEEN ANNE

Spanning most of the first half of the 18th Century, the Queen Anne style was both influential and original, characterized by refined, flowing lines without excessive decoration. In chair and table making, the style spawned an important innovation: the cabriole leg. Queen Anne designs migrated to America after becoming well established in England. The style eventually found a home in Philadelphia, the colonies' most important cabinet-making center. Queen Anne furniture remained popular in America long after it was superceded in England by the early Georgian style.

SECRETARY
(page 104)
A desk-bookcase combination with a veneered fall-front; features dovetailed corners and drawers

Large brass back plate with bail

QUEEN ANNE CHAIR

Curved chair back

Padded slip seat

Cabriole leg

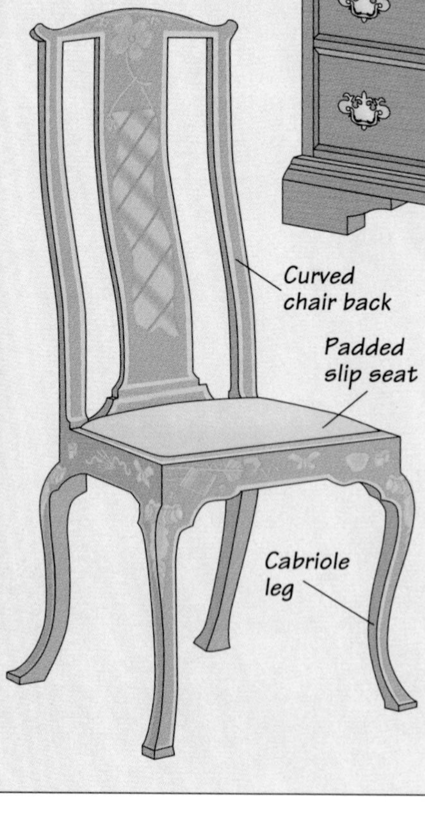

CARD TABLE
Top folds in half and side rails fold inward to move legs closer together

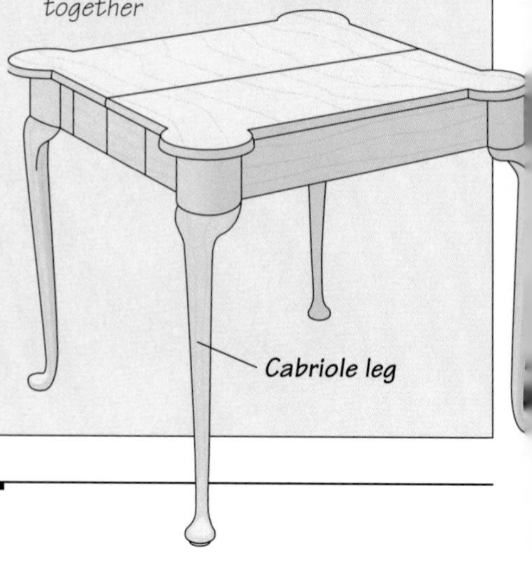

Cabriole leg

The highboy above exemplifies the harmony between straight lines and fluid curves typical of Queen Anne-style furniture

CHIPPENDALE

Named after British master carver and furniture designer Thomas Chippendale, this style emerged in the second half of the 18th Century. It is often thought of as Queen Anne dressed up with ornamentation such as shell carvings, intricate fretwork, piecrust edging, and other elements of rococo or Chinese design. The style flourished in the American cabinet-making centers of Boston, New York, Newport, and Philadelphia, with each center developing its own signature. Philadelphia Chippendale was the most extravagent in its carved detail, while in New York the style was more restrained. In Boston, the bombé-shaped chest was popular. Newport helped popularize a uniquely American form: the block-front.

CHINESE CHIPPENDALE CHAIR
Featured a clean rectangular look with light geometric fretwork

Geometric fretwork

Piecrust edging

Rococo carvings

TEA TABLE
Featured a tilting top and tripod legs

SATINWOOD COMMODE
The bombé shape was typical of the Boston style

Rosette pull

Shell carving

Applied molding

BLOCK-FRONT CHEST
An American adaption of the Chippendale style

FEDERAL PERIOD

After the Revolution, American furniture makers began to distance themselves from British influence. Endeavoring to create a new style, they turned to the classical designs of ancient Greece and Rome. For this reason, Federal furniture is often called "Neoclassical." More austere than Chippendale, Federal pieces typically mimicked the lines and features of antiquity, such as columns, animal claws, reeding, fluting, and the lyre.

Despite efforts to achieve independence, however, American cabinetmakers remained under British influence. The designs of Englishmen George Hepplewhite and Thomas Sheraton were widely circulated and copied in America, although some New World designers attempted to Americanize the British styles by incorporating the eagle and other patriotic motifs.

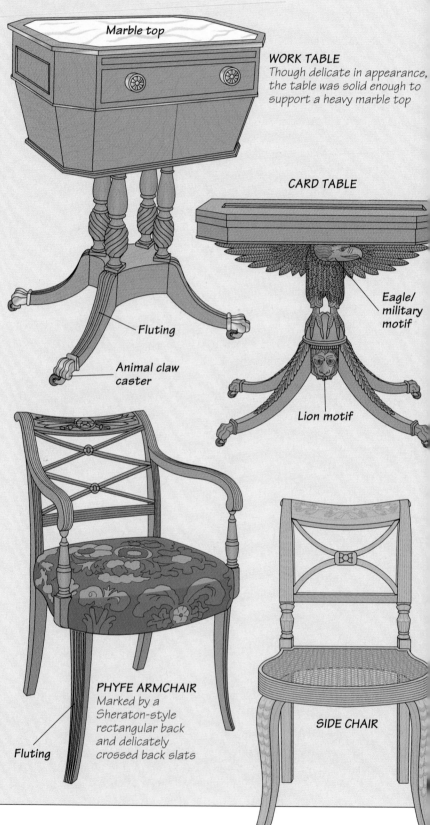

Marble top

WORK TABLE
Though delicate in appearance, the table was solid enough to support a heavy marble top

CARD TABLE

Fluting

Animal claw caster

Eagle/ military motif

Lion motif

PHYFE ARMCHAIR
Marked by a Sheraton-style rectangular back and delicately crossed back slats

Fluting

SIDE CHAIR

Designed to fit below a recessed window, the aptly named window seat, like the one shown above, was a popular Federal period design. The cross-lattice pattern of the raised ends is typical of the best-known Federal designer, Duncan Phyfe.

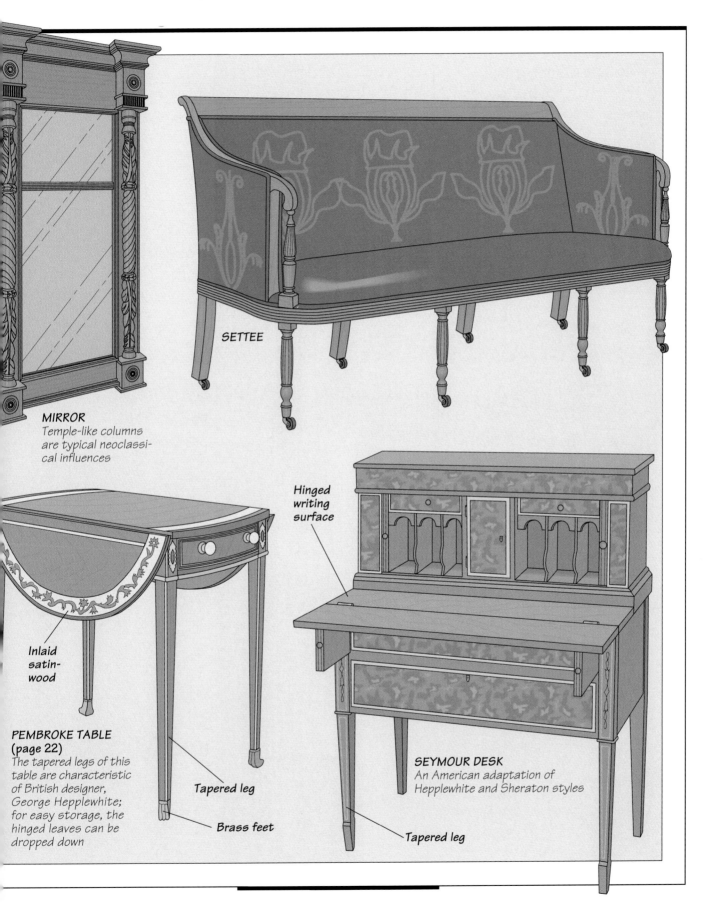

SETTEE

MIRROR
Temple-like columns are typical neoclassical influences

Hinged writing surface

Inlaid satinwood

PEMBROKE TABLE (page 22)
The tapered legs of this table are characteristic of British designer, George Hepplewhite; for easy storage, the hinged leaves can be dropped down

Tapered leg

Brass feet

SEYMOUR DESK
An American adaptation of Hepplewhite and Sheraton styles

Tapered leg

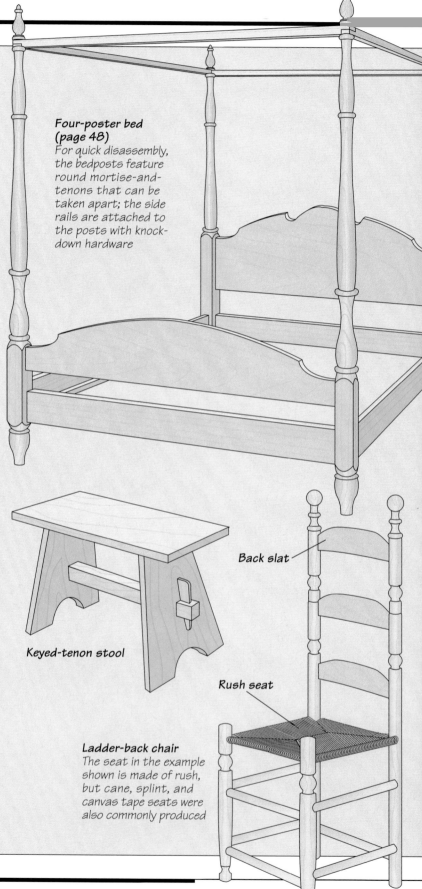

AMERICAN COUNTRY/COLONIAL

Using local wood species and unsophisticated construction methods, colonial America's pioneers adapted traditional country designs from England to produce simple, practical furniture known as American Country.

Although more sophisticated styles supplanted these designs in prosperous colonial towns, rustic furniture prevailed on the ever-advancing frontier. With its simplicity, durability, and economy, traditional American Country furniture continues to appeal to 20th-Century furniture makers, particularly those living in rural America.

Four-poster bed (page 48)
For quick disassembly, the bedposts feature round mortise-and-tenons that can be taken apart; the side rails are attached to the posts with knock-down hardware

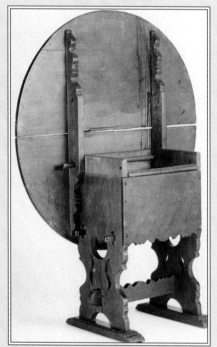

An ingenious response to cramped conditions, the chair table shown above serves double duty. With the tilted-up top against a wall, the piece can be used as a chair. Lowering the top transforms it into a table.

Keyed-tenon stool

Back slat

Rush seat

Ladder-back chair
The seat in the example shown is made of rush, but cane, splint, and canvas tape seats were also commonly produced

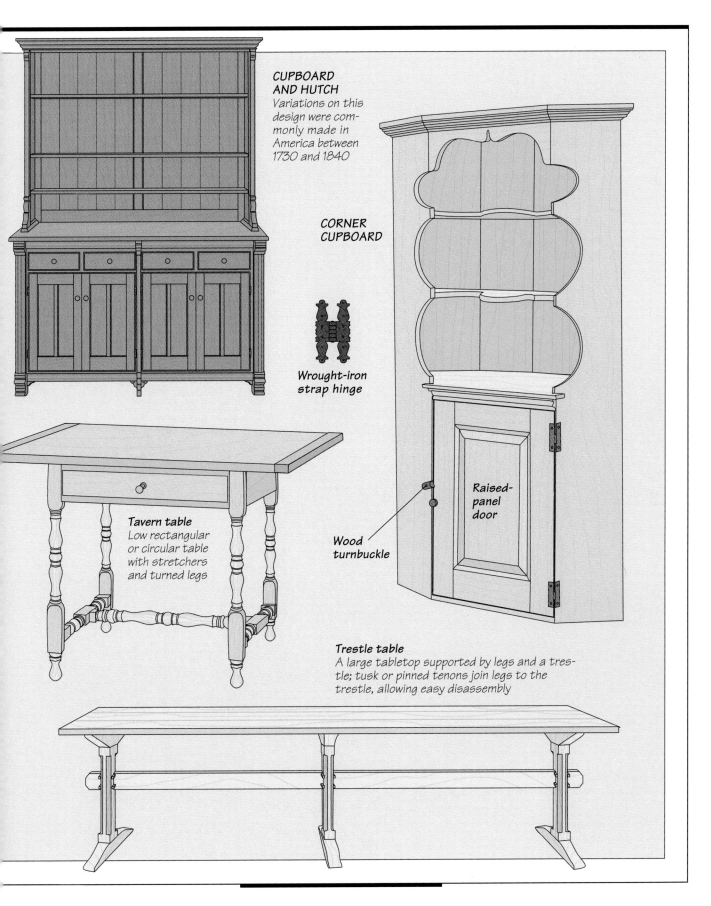

CUPBOARD AND HUTCH
Variations on this design were commonly made in America between 1730 and 1840

CORNER CUPBOARD

Wrought-iron strap hinge

Raised-panel door

Wood turnbuckle

Tavern table
Low rectangular or circular table with stretchers and turned legs

Trestle table
A large tabletop supported by legs and a trestle; tusk or pinned tenons join legs to the trestle, allowing easy disassembly

WINDSOR

The Windsor chair *(page 70)* is often classified with American Country furniture because its simple and precise joinery and functional elegance harken back to the craftsmanship of a bygone era. But the Windsor is neither American nor rural. First made in late 17th-Century England, it is one of the most enduring and popular of all chair designs. The Windsor family also includes stools, cradles, stands, and tables.

Although the Windsor chair has spawned countless variations, virtually all versions feature a solid seat, which anchors separate assemblies of turned legs and a spindle back.

Many of the elements of the comb-back Windsor chair shown above were riven and shaped from green wood. The chair was made by North Carolina woodworker Drew Langsner.

CONTINUOUS-ARM CHAIR
Features a single continuous arm made of steamed wood supported by turned spindles and arm posts

Spindle

Arm

Bracing stick

Turned leg and stretcher

HIGH CHAIR

OVAL-BACK CHAIR

Sculpted seat

SETTEE

REGIONAL STYLES

Like the early settlers from England, newcomers to America from other parts of the world brought their unique cabinetmaking traditions with them. From the Dutch who founded New Amsterdam to the Zoarite Germans who settled in Ohio, the new arrivals added their own influence to the catalog of early American styles. Mixed into the blend were North American versions of national styles built in the former French and Spanish colonies. The pieces shown here are a brief sampling of regional styles.

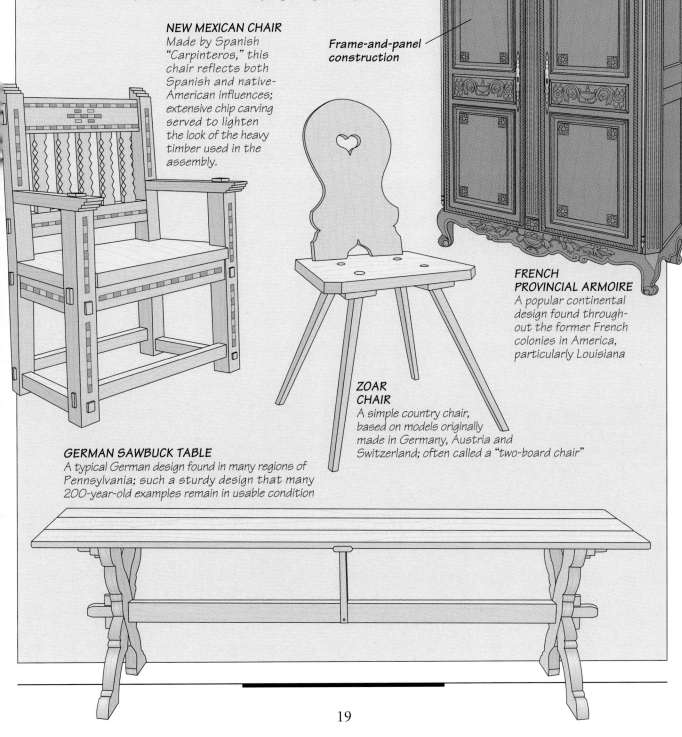

NEW MEXICAN CHAIR
Made by Spanish "Carpinteros," this chair reflects both Spanish and native-American influences; extensive chip carving served to lighten the look of the heavy timber used in the assembly.

Frame-and-panel construction

FRENCH PROVINCIAL ARMOIRE
A popular continental design found throughout the former French colonies in America, particularly Louisiana

ZOAR CHAIR
A simple country chair, based on models originally made in Germany, Austria and Switzerland; often called a "two-board chair"

GERMAN SAWBUCK TABLE
A typical German design found in many regions of Pennsylvania; such a sturdy design that many 200-year-old examples remain in usable condition

SHAKER

The Shakers were a puritanical religious sect that prospered in the 1800s, mainly in New England, New York State, and the Midwest. They lived in isolation from society on self-sufficient farms. Shaker furniture is practical, functional, and austere—without extravagance or ornamentation—but attractive in its simplicity. Shaker design principles continue to inspire modern funiture makers.

Like other Shaker pieces, the drop-leaf table shown above owes its beauty to its clean lines and complete devotion to function. With its leaves extended, the table can seat four people. When the entire surface is not needed, the leaves can be dropped down and the table stored compactly up against a wall.

STEP STOOL
Assembled with through dovetails, these mini-stepladders enabled Shakers to reach the top shelves and doors of floor-to-ceiling casework; three- and four-step versions were also common

ROCKING CHAIR
Has steam-bent rear legs and solid-wood rockers; the tape seating is available in a variety of colors and patterns. Also made in a ladder-back version

BLANKET CHEST
For storing blankets and quilts

PIE SAFE
Traditionally used to store baked goods; the pierced-tin door panels kept the contents fresh while preventing vermin from entering. Adjustable shelves added flexibility

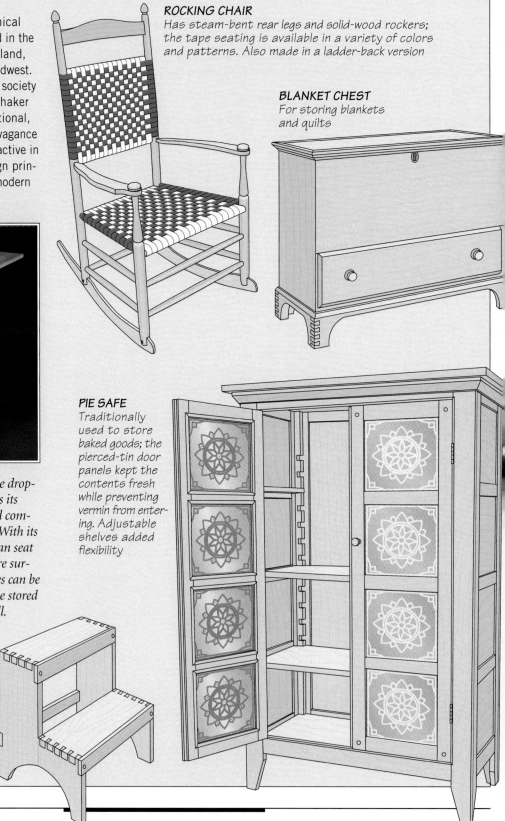

MISSION

The Mission style is an offshoot of the Arts and Crafts movement that evolved in England as a reaction to the stylistic excesses of the Victorian period and to the decline in craftsmanship caused by the Industrial Revolution. Led by designers like Gustav Stickley, American furniture makers adopted preindustrial work methods to create functional, unadorned furniture. Mission-style pieces featured exposed joints, native wood species (often oak) and a generally more rustic look. Mission furniture greatly influenced major architects such as Charles and Henry Greene and Frank Lloyd Wright

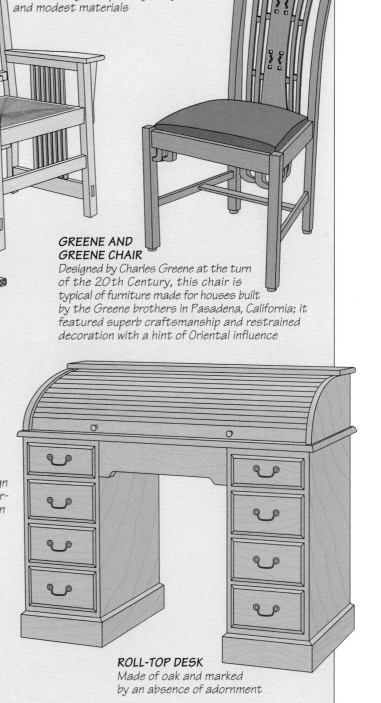

MISSION ARMCHAIR
Gustav Stickley sought to create simple, durable and comfortable furniture; this piece features straightforward, rectilinear designs, exposed joinery and modest materials

GREENE AND GREENE CHAIR
Designed by Charles Greene at the turn of the 20th Century, this chair is typical of furniture made for houses built by the Greene brothers in Pasadena, California; it featured superb craftsmanship and restrained decoration with a hint of Oriental influence

ARTS AND CRAFTS OAK TABLE
The solid, handcrafted stretcher borrows its design from the sturdy undercarriage of a farm hay wagon

STICKLEY ROCKING CHAIR
Built from solid oak, this chair features inlaid floral motifs on the back slats than enrich an otherwise austere piece

ROLL-TOP DESK
Made of oak and marked by an absence of adornment

PEMBROKE TABLE

The legs of the Pembroke table feature strips of dark banding, framed by thin string inlay of a lighter wood.

The Pembroke table is thought to have originated in the mid-18th Century, when Lady Pembroke commissioned the great Georgian cabinetmaker and master carver Thomas Chippendale to fashion a small casual table for her. The example featured in this chapter, however, has more in common with the neoclassical designs of Sheraton and American Federal furniture, which flourished in the following century. Its graceful blend of straight lines and gentle curves contrasts sharply with the intricate and ornate rococo designs of Chippendale.

The earliest versions of this piece were built at a time when space was at a premium in most homes and furniture had to occupy as little room as possible. The Pembroke table meets this challenge in a couple of ingenious ways. First, the table's top is flanked by two leaves that can be raised up when the entire table surface is needed and then lowered when it is not, allowing the table to be stored compactly in a corner or hallway. The leaves are attached to the top with a hinged joint known as a rule joint. As shown beginning on page 43, matching cove and round-over bits are used in a table-mounted router to shape the edges of the top and leaves. Rule-joint hinges are then recessed into the undersides of the panels to complete the connection. The leaves are supported in their extended position by fly rails attached to the side rails with knuckle joints *(page 32)*.

Another of the table's functional features is the drawer that slides under the top. Perfect for storing utensils and linens, the drawer is made with through dovetails. The end grain of the sides is concealed by a false front, which is curved to match the curved rail at the table's other end.

In keeping with the table's straight and elegant lines, the legs are simply tapered on four sides *(page 26)*. Narrow strips of banding near the legs' bottom ends *(page 27)* add a decorative touch.

The joinery used to assemble the table is sturdy and relatively simple. The rails are fixed to the legs with blind mortise-and-tenons *(page 33)*, reinforced by wooden corner blocks. The drawer rails attach to the legs with two different joints: dovetailed half-laps at the top and twin mortise-and-tenon joints on the bottom.

Made from mahogany with contrasting walnut and maple inlay around the legs, the Pembroke table shown at left is an elegant piece of furniture with several useful features, including drop leaves on the sides and a drawer at one end.

ANATOMY OF A PEMBROKE TABLE

The Pembroke table consists of three main sections: a top, the leg-and-rail assembly, and a drawer. The top is attached to a leaf on each side with a hinged rule joint. The edges of the top are rounded over and the matching edges of the leaves are shaped with a matching cove, forming a seamless joint when the leaves are in the up position. The leaves are supported by fly rails that swing out from the side rails on knuckle joints. As shown opposite, these joints feature interlocking fingers fixed together by a wooden pin.

Each side rail is made up of four individual boards. First, the knuckle joint between the long outer side rail piece

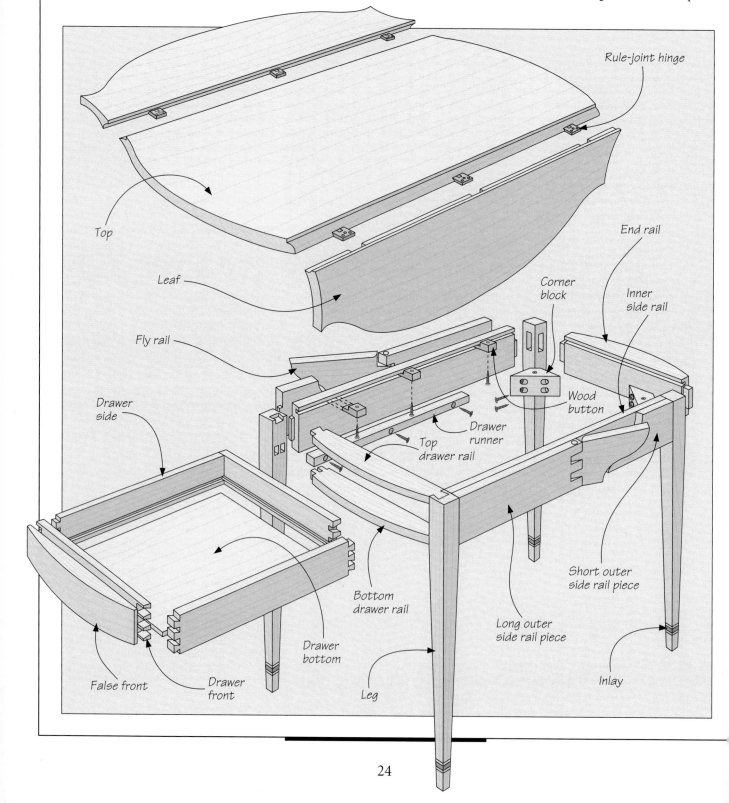

Rule-joint hinge

Top

Leaf

Fly rail

End rail

Corner block

Inner side rail

Drawer side

Wood button

Drawer runner

Top drawer rail

Bottom drawer rail

Drawer bottom

Short outer side rail piece

Long outer side rail piece

False front

Drawer front

Leg

Inlay

and the fly rail is cut and assembled. Then, the short outer side rail piece is sawn to size and the stationary pieces are face-glued to the inner side rail. The assembly is then joined to the legs with blind mortise-and-tenons. Wooden cor-ner blocks are screwed to adjoining rails at the back end of the table to keep the corners square.

The top is attached to the rails with wood buttons, which feature a lip that fits into a groove cut along the inside edges of the rails; the buttons are screwed to the underside of the top. As shown on page 47, pocket holes can also be used.

The dovetailed drawer is supported by wooden runners screwed flush with the bottom edge of the side rails.

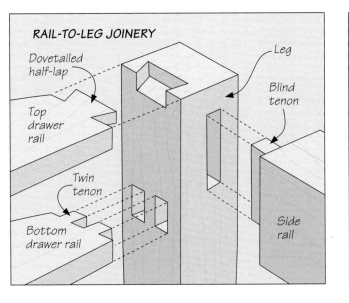

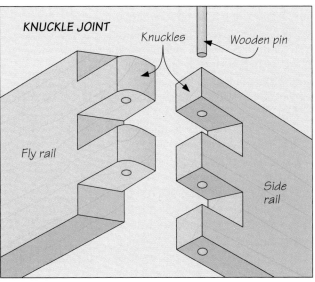

CUTTING LIST

ITEM		QUANTITY	THICKNESS	WIDTH	LENGTH
Corner blocks		2	3"	3"	3"
Drawer:	Front and back	2	⅝"	2⅞"	14⅞"
	False front	1	1½"	2⅞"	14⅞"
	Sides	2	⅝"	2⅞"	18"
	Drawer rails*	2	¾"	3"	16⅜"
	Runners	2	¾"	1"	21"
	Bottom	1	¼"	14"	17¼"
End rail*		1	4⅜"	3"	16⅜"
Fly rails		2	1"	4⅜"	10½"
Inner side rails*		2	1"	4⅜"	32"
Leaves		2	⅞"	10"	41"
Legs		4	1¾"	1¾"	29¼"
Short outer side rail pieces*		2	1"	4⅜"	11¼"
Long outer side rail pieces*		2	1"	4⅜"	16¾"
Top		1	⅞"	20"	41"

*Note: Dimensions include tenon or half-lap lengths.

MAKING THE LEG-AND-RAIL ASSEMBLY

The legs of a Pembroke table have a delicate look that belies their sturdiness. They are tapered, with a simple banded inlay around each leg about 3 inches from the bottom. The banding includes a ¾-inch-wide dark strip—in this case, walnut—which contrasts with the mahogany. A thin strip of maple frames the walnut. On some Pembroke tables, the inlay was used to mark the transition to a second, steeper taper at the bottom of the leg. Traditionally, legs with a double taper were tapered on the two inside faces above the banding and on all four sides below it. The version shown in this chapter features a single taper on each face.

Once the side rails are assembled, they are joined to the legs with mortise- and-tenons *(page 33)*. So, too, is the end rail, but it must first be bandsawed into a curved shape to complement the curved drawer front at the opposite end of the table *(page 36)*. The drawer rails are fixed to the legs with twin mortise-and-tenons and dovetailed half-laps *(page 34)*.

A fly rail holds up one of the leaves of the Pembroke table shown above. The knuckle joint that attaches the fly rail to the side rail is designed to stop pivoting once the fly rail opens to a 90° angle. A recess carved into the curved edge of the fly rail provides a convenient handhold.

TAPERING THE LEGS

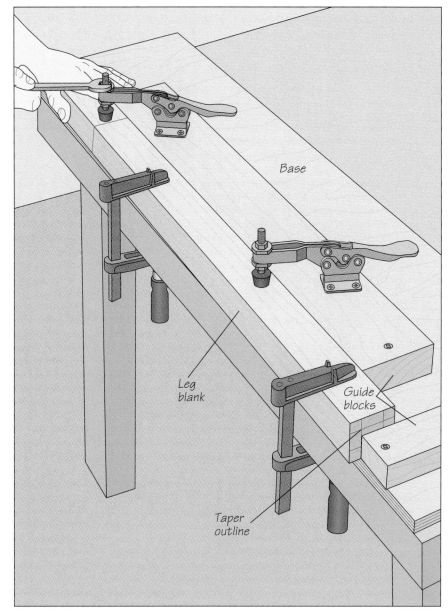

Base

Leg blank

Guide blocks

Taper outline

1 Making a taper jig

Cut your leg blanks to size, referring to the anatomy illustration on page 24. Mark a line all around each blank 5 inches from the top end to define the square section to which the rails will be joined. Then outline a ¾-inch square on the bottom end of the blank to define the taper. To make the cut on your table saw, use a shop-made jig. Cut the base from ¾-inch plywood, making it longer and wider than the blanks. Set a blank on the base, aligning corresponding taper lines at the top and bottom with the edge of the base. Clamp the blank in place and position the guide blocks against it. Screw the guide blocks to the base, then fasten two toggle clamps to the longer block. Press the toggle clamps down to secure the blank to the jig, tightening the nuts on the clamps with a wrench *(above)*. Remove the bar clamps.

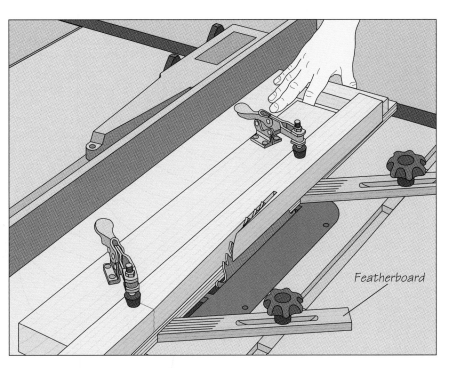

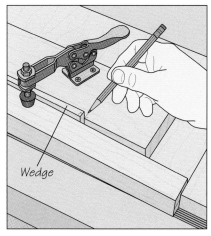

Wedge

3 Cutting the remaining tapers
Release the toggle clamps, turn the blank to the adjacent side, and reclamp it, this time using a wedge between the long guide block and the tapered part of the blank to compensate for the cut you just made. Mark the location of the broad end of the wedge on the guide block so you can reposition the wedge properly for the remaining two cuts *(above)*. Then taper the second side of the blank. Repeat the process for the remaining sides.

2 Cutting the first taper
Butt the edge of the jig base with the blank against the blade and position the rip fence flush against the opposite edge of the base. To support the blank during the cut, mount two featherboards to the saw table, one on each side of the blade. Taper the first side of the blank by sliding the jig and workpiece across the table, making sure neither hand is in line with the blade *(above)*. **(Caution: Blade guard removed for clarity.)**

Featherboard

INSTALLING INLAY BANDING ON THE LEGS

Miter gauge extension

Leg

Miter bar

Try square blade

1 Setting up the router table
To cut dadoes in the legs for inlay banding on a router table, install a ¾-inch straight bit in a router and mount the tool in a table. Adjust the cutter for a ⅛-inch-deep cut. Next, attach an extension board to the miter gauge. To ensure that the dadoes are parallel to the ends of the leg, the miter gauge must be set to the appropriate angle. Hold the tapered part of the leg flush against the miter gauge extension while butting the handle of a try square against the leg's square portion. Adjust the miter gauge so the miter bar is parallel to the blade of the square *(left)*.

2 Routing the dadoes

Position the leg against the miter gauge extension so the bottom end is 3³/₁₆ inch to the right of the bit. To ensure all the dadoes will be aligned, butt a stop block against the end of the leg and clamp it to the extension. To cut the first dado, hold the leg flush against the extension and stop block, and feed the leg and miter gauge across the table into the bit. Turn the blank to the adjacent side and repeat to rout the remaining dadoes *(left)*.

Stop block

3 Gluing the banding

Using a hardwood darker than the leg, cut a rectangular piece of banding for every dado. Saw the banding so the grain will be parallel with the grain of the leg when the pieces are glued in place; they should be the same width as the dadoes, but about ¼ inch longer and ³/₁₆ inch thick. Spread glue on two pieces of banding, set them in dadoes on opposite sides of the leg and secure them in place with a C clamp *(right)*. Once the adhesive has cured, remove the clamp and trim the ends of the banding flush with the leg by running the adjoining dadoes across the router table again as in step 2. Glue banding into these dadoes, then sand the banding flush with the leg surface.

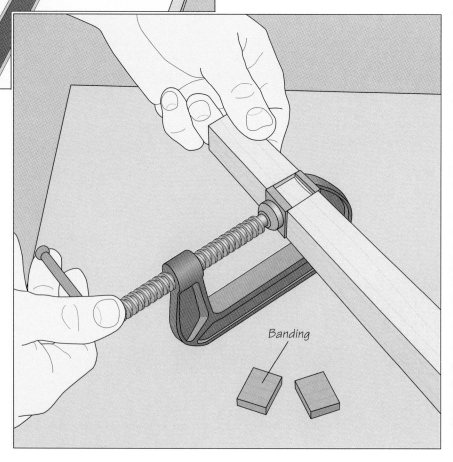

Banding

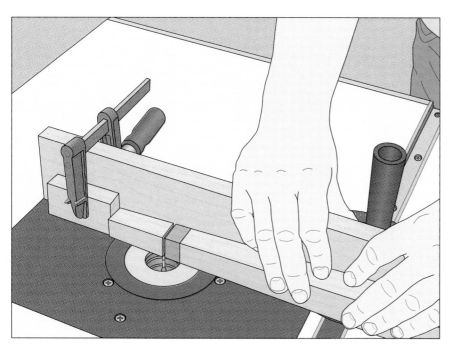

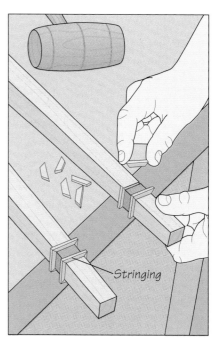

4 Kerfing the legs for the stringing

To accentuate the inlay banding on the legs, install narrow strips of wood called stringing between the banding and the leg. For maximum effect, choose a species that is lighter than the wood you have selected for the table. Using the same procedure you followed in step 2, cut slots for the stringing along the edges of the banding—but this time, with a ⅛-inch upcut spiral straight bit in the router. Cut all the slots at the bottom edge of the banding first, then reposition the stop block to rout the remaining slots.

5 Installing the stringing

Make the stringing from ⅛-inch-thick, ¼-inch wide wood strips. Using a backsaw in a mini-miter box (like the kind used in dollhouse-building), cut the strips to fit in the slots. Cut and fit one piece at a time, mitering the ends at 45°. Apply glue to the piece, insert it into its slot *(above)* and tap it into place with a wooden mallet. Once all the stringing is installed and the adhesive has cured, sand the pieces flush with the leg surfaces.

Instead of being cut to fit into a dado in a leg, the commercial inlay veneers shown at left are glued to the sides of a tapered leg blank.

MAKING THE SIDE RAILS

1 Marking the knuckle joints
Butt the mating ends of the fly rail and the long outer side rail piece together, making sure the board edges are aligned. Use reference letters to label the pieces, then mark a shoulder line on each board about 1 inch from their mating ends; use a try square to ensure the lines are perpendicular to the board edges. To complete the joint outline, use a tape measure to divide the boards into five equal segments across their width, creating a grid of fingers and notches on the board ends. Mark the waste sections—or notches—with Xs *(right)* so the fly rail will have three notches and the mating piece two notches.

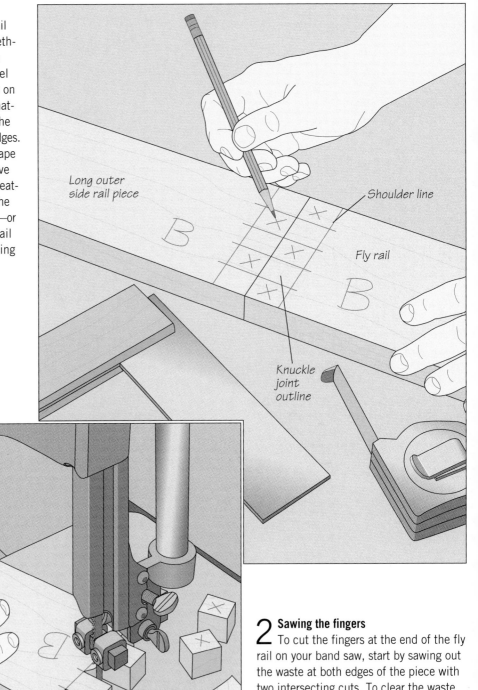

Long outer side rail piece

Shoulder line

Fly rail

Knuckle joint outline

Fly rail

Finger

2 Sawing the fingers
To cut the fingers at the end of the fly rail on your band saw, start by sawing out the waste at both edges of the piece with two intersecting cuts. To clear the waste between the fingers, nibble at it with the blade, pivoting the piece as necessary to avoid cutting into the fingers *(left)*. Once all the fingers are cut, test-fit the joint and make any necessary adjustments with a chisel.

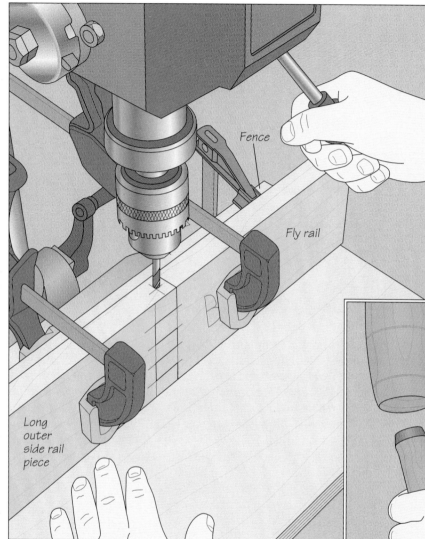

Fence

Fly rail

Long
outer
side rail
piece

3 Drilling the pin holes

Assemble each of the knuckle joints, then mark the center of the fingers on the top edge of the long rail piece. Bore the hole for the wooden pin on your drill press. Install a ¼-inch bit in the machine and clamp a backup panel to the table. Set the boards on the panel, aligning the center mark directly under the bit. Clamp a board against the back face of the stock, then secure it to the backup panel as a fence. Drill right through the stock *(left)*. If the bit is not long enough to penetrate to the other edge of the boards, turn the stock over and complete the hole from the other side.

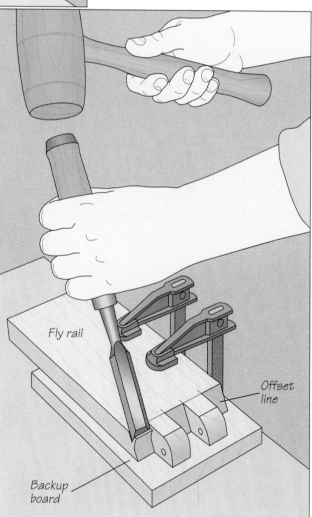

Fly rail

Offset
line

Backup
board

4 Fine-tuning the knuckle joints

If the shoulders and fingers of the knuckle joints were left square, the fly rails would bind against the side rails when they were extended. To permit the joints to pivot, mark a line on the inside face of each fly rail and side rail piece parallel to the shoulder line and offset ½ inch from it. Clamp one fly rail inside-face up on a work surface with a backup board between the rail and the table. Start by using a chisel the same width as the fingers and notches to round over the end of the fingers. Then position the tip of the chisel blade on the offset line, centered on a notch, angling the tool so the cut will end at the original shoulder line. Holding the chisel with one hand, tap it with a wooden mallet to bevel the shoulder. Repeat for the remaining notches *(right)*. Bevel the notches the same way on the long rail piece, but leave the fingers square.

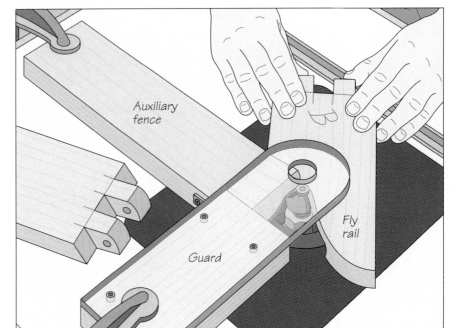

5 Cutting the fly rails to length

Refer to the anatomy illustration *(page 24)* to mark the S-shaped cutting line on the fly rails, then designate the waste with Xs. Feed the stock across the band saw table *(above)*, making certain neither hand is in line with the blade. Make matching cuts on the mating ends of the short outer rail pieces, ensuring that there will be a sufficiently large gap—about ½ inch—between the two boards for a handhold.

7 Gluing up the side rails

Assemble the knuckle joints, inserting lengths of ¼-inch dowel into the holes through the fingers, and cut the inner side rail pieces to length. For each side rail, spread glue on the contacting surfaces of the boards and clamp the outer rail pieces to the inner rail; do not apply any glue on the fly rail since it must be free to pivot. Make sure to leave a ½-inch gap between the fly rail and the short outer side rail piece. Alternate the clamps across the top and bottom edges of the assembly, spacing them 3 to 4 inches apart. Tighten the clamps evenly *(right)* until adhesive squeezes out of the joints.

6 Routing finger recesses in the fly rails

To facilitate pivoting the fly rails, cut finger recesses into the underside of their curved ends. Install a piloted cove bit in a router, mount the tool in a table, and set the cutting depth at ⅝ inch. To provide a bearing surface for the rails, fashion a fence for the stock to ride against on the infeed side of the table and a guard for the bit from a ply-wood block and clear acrylic. Attach the guard and fence together and clamp them to the table. Press the stock against the pilot bearing as you feed each rail across the table *(above)*; make the recess about 4 inches long and center it on the rail's curved end.

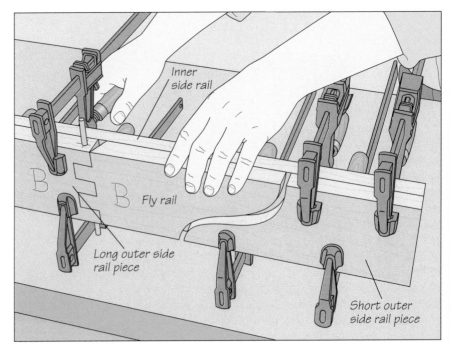

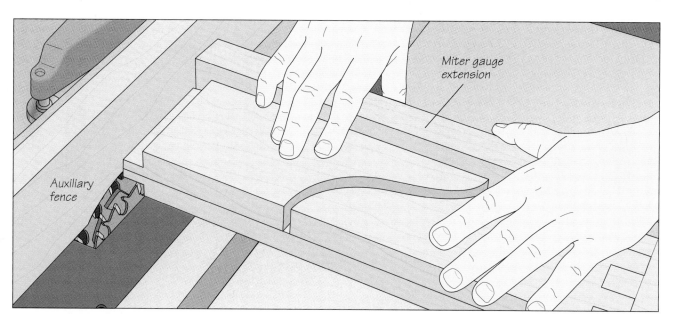

8 Cutting the rail tenons

The next step in making the rails is to cut the tenons that will fit into the leg mortises. Start by drilling a test mortise *(page 37)*, then outline the tenons on the ends of the rails, using the test mortise as a guide. Cut the tenons on your table saw fitted with a dado head; adjust the width of the head to slightly more than the tenon length—about ¾ inch. Set the cutting height at one-third the stock thickness. Attach an auxiliary fence to the saw's rip fence and an extension board to the miter gauge. To position the fence, align the shoulder line on the rail with the dado head and butt the fence against the end of the board. Feed the rail face down, holding the stock flush against the fence and the miter gauge extension. Turn the rail over and repeat the cut on the other side *(above)*, fitting the tenon in the test mortise and raising the blades until the fit is snug. Cut tenon cheeks at the other end and repeat for each side and end rail. Next, flip the rail on edge and adjust the blade height to trim the tenons to width. Again, test the tenon until it fits snugly in the trial mortise.

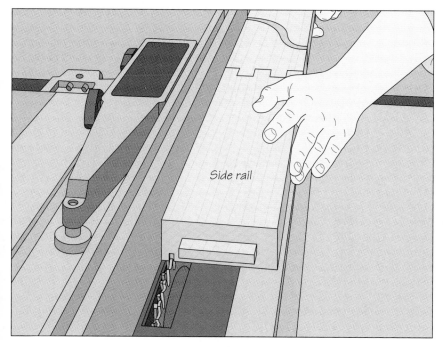

9 Preparing the rails for the top

Once all the tenons are finished, you will need to cut a groove along the inside face of the rails to accommodate the wood buttons that will secure the tabletop in place. Leave the dado head on your table saw, adjust its width to ¼ inch, and set the cutting height at about ⅞ inch. Position the fence about ¾ inch from the blades. Feed the rails into the dado head inside-face down and with the top edge pressed against the fence *(left)*. Also cut a groove in the end rail blank at this time. This will ensure that all the grooves are identical. **(Caution: Blade guard removed for clarity.)**

PREPARING THE DRAWER RAILS AND END RAIL

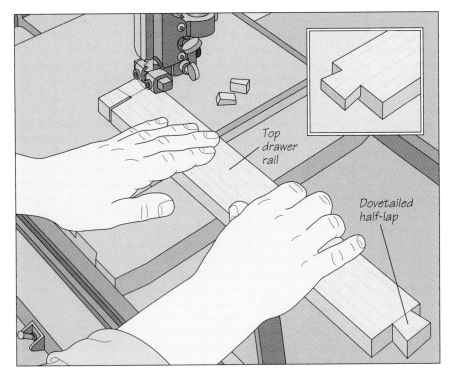

Top drawer rail

Dovetailed half-lap

1 Cutting the top drawer rail
Cut the top drawer rail to length, then outline the dovetailed half-laps that will join the ends of the rail to the front legs of the table. Offset the outline toward the back edge of the rail so the dovetail will be centered on the leg when the rail's back edge is flush with the back face of the leg *(step 2)*. Cut out the dovetails on your band saw, making two intersecting cuts along each edge of the outlines *(left)*. Then use your table saw fitted with a dado head to cut away one-half the thickness of the dovetails from their bottom face *(inset)*.

2 Cutting the dovetail sockets in the legs
Secure a front leg upright in a bench vise and use one of the dovetailed half-laps you cut in step 1 to outline the mating socket on the leg's top end. Make sure the top end of the leg is flush with the benchtop; this will support the router base plate as you cut the socket. Also ensure that the dovetail shoulder is butted against the inside edge of the leg and the rail's back edge is flush with the back face of the leg as you mark the lines. Install a ⅛-inch upcut-spiral straight bit into a router and adjust the cutting depth to the thickness of the dovetail. Rout the socket within the marked outline, then square the corners and pare to the line with straight and skew chisels, as needed. Repeat to cut the socket in the other front leg *(right)*.

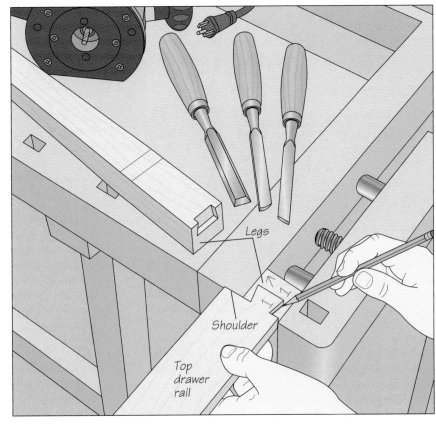

Legs

Shoulder

Top drawer rail

3 Cutting twin tenons in the bottom drawer rail

The bottom drawer rail is joined to the legs with twin mortise-and-tenon joints. Cut the tenons at the ends of the rail on your table saw. Install a dado head ¾ inch wide, then set up a tenoning jig in the miter slot. Mark a twin tenon at each end of the rail and set the cutting height at ¾ inch. Lay out the tenons so the back edges of the rail and leg will align *(step 4)*. Clamp the rail end-up in the jig, placing a shim between the two to prevent the dado head from contacting the jig. Shift the jig sideways to align one of the tenon marks with the dado head. To make the cut, push the jig forward, feeding the stock into the blades. Shift the jig to line up the dado head with the waste adjoining the twin tenons, making several passes until you have cleared away the excess wood *(right)*. Repeat the cut at the other end of the rail.

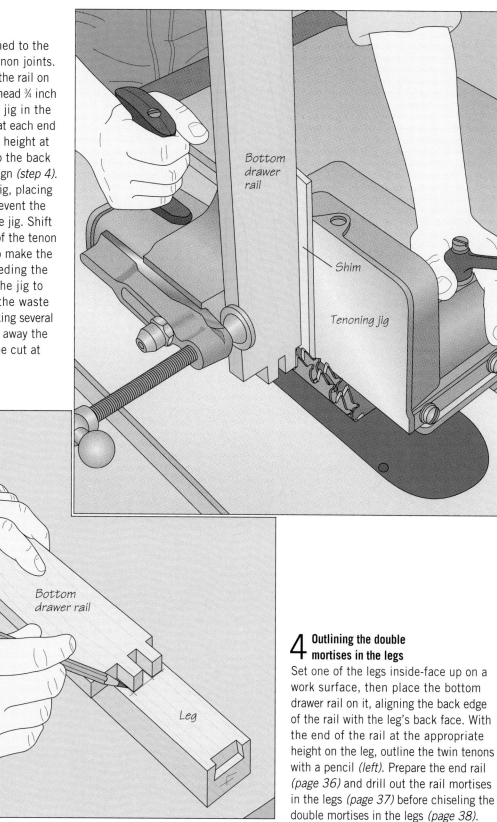

4 Outlining the double mortises in the legs

Set one of the legs inside-face up on a work surface, then place the bottom drawer rail on it, aligning the back edge of the rail with the leg's back face. With the end of the rail at the appropriate height on the leg, outline the twin tenons with a pencil *(left)*. Prepare the end rail *(page 36)* and drill out the rail mortises in the legs *(page 37)* before chiseling the double mortises in the legs *(page 38)*.

5 Cutting the curved face of the end rail

Outline the curved outside face of the end rail on the edges so the legs will extend ¼ inch beyond the rail when the table is assembled. Then, standing at the side of the band saw table, set the rail down on edge. Align the blade just to the waste side of the cutting line near the center and hold the two ends to feed the stock across the table; make sure neither hand is in line with the blade. Once one waste piece falls away, turn the rail over and cut the opposite end *(right)*.

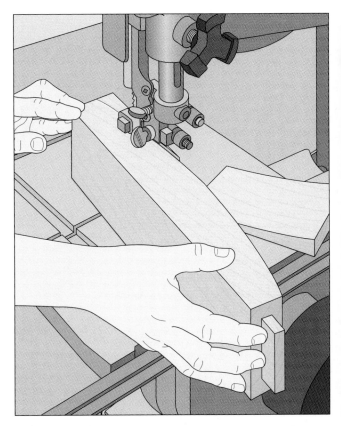

6 Veneering the end rail

If your end rail was made from glued-up stock, you may need to apply a piece of veneer to the outside face to conceal any glues lines that might be visible. Follow the same procedures you would use on the fall-front of a slant-top desk. Make the veneer pattern and set up a vacuum press *(page 123)*. For the model shown, insert the hose into the nipple in the bottom of the press bag. Then place the platen in the bag and slide the nipple into the platen sleeve. Set the end rail on a work surface, apply the glue, and lay the veneer on the rail. Place a piece of wax paper over the veneer, rest the caul on top, and place the assembly atop the platen. Seal the bag, turn on the pump and leave the assembly under pressure for the recommended length of time *(below)*. Most vacuum presses will shut off when the appropriate pressure has been reached.

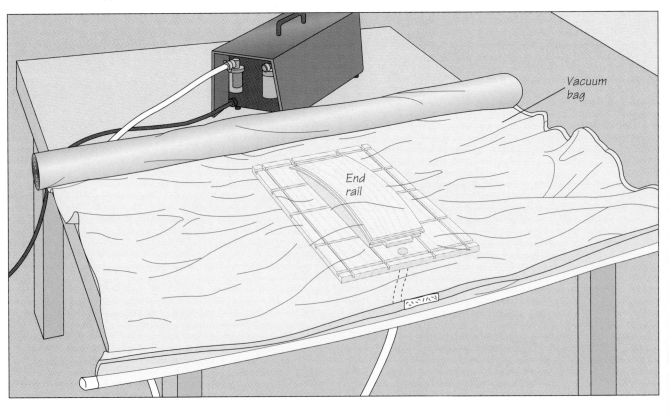

Vacuum bag

End rail

GLUING UP THE LEGS AND RAILS

1 **Outlining the rail mortises in the legs**
Use one of the rail tenons you cut *(page 33)* to outline the length and width of the mortises. Start by holding the cheek of the tenon flush against the inside face of one of the legs; make sure that the top edge of the rail is aligned with the top end of the leg. Mark the length of the mortise. To outline the mortise width, hold the edge of the tenon flush against the inside face of the leg and mark the cheeks of the tenon *(right)*. Extend the lines along the face (shown in the illustration as dotted lines). Repeat for the remaining side and end rail mortises. Remember that the outside face of the legs should extend beyond the end rail by about ¼ inch.

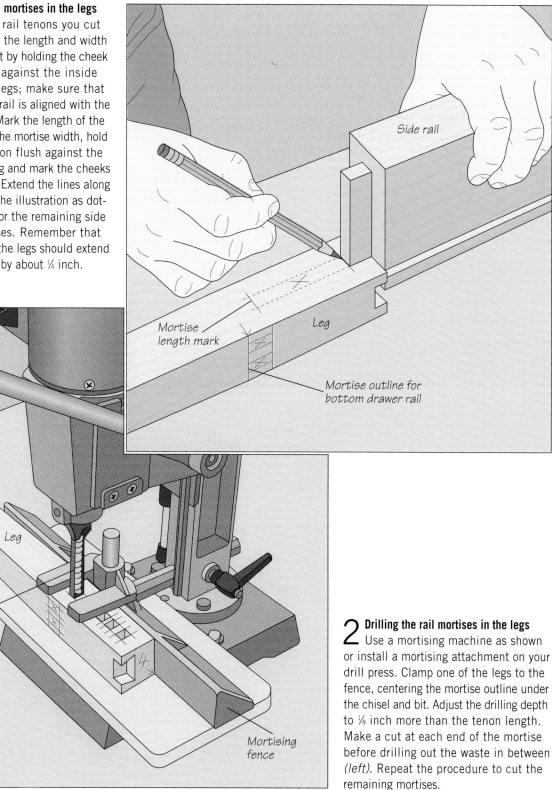

Side rail

Mortise
length mark

Leg

Mortise outline for
bottom drawer rail

Leg

Chisel
and bit

Mortising
fence

2 **Drilling the rail mortises in the legs**
Use a mortising machine as shown or install a mortising attachment on your drill press. Clamp one of the legs to the fence, centering the mortise outline under the chisel and bit. Adjust the drilling depth to ⅛ inch more than the tenon length. Make a cut at each end of the mortise before drilling out the waste in between *(left)*. Repeat the procedure to cut the remaining mortises.

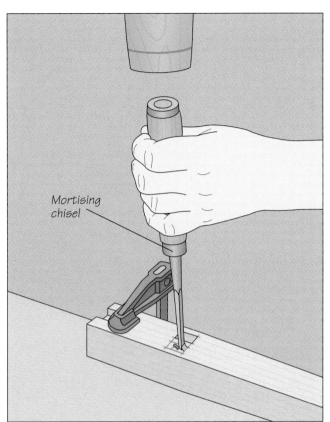

Mortising
chisel

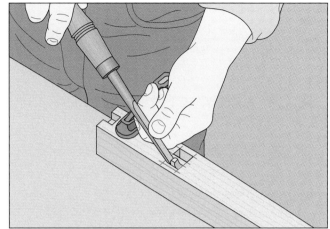

3 **Chiseling the double mortises for the bottom drawer rail**
Clamp a leg inside-face up to a work surface. Then, starting at one end of the double mortise outline, hold a mortising
chisel square to the inside face of the leg and strike the handle
with a wooden mallet *(left)*. Use a chisel the same width as the
mortises and be sure that the beveled side is facing the waste.
Continue making cuts at intervals of about ⅛ inch until you
reach the other end of the outline. Use the chisel to lever out
the waste to the required depth *(above)*. Chop out the remaining
double mortises the same way. Test-fit the joints and widen or
deepen the mortises with the chisel, as required.

4 **Gluing the legs to the side rails**
Test-assemble the legs and side rails,
fine-tuning any ill-fitting joints with a
chisel, if necessary. Sand any surfaces
that will be difficult to access once the
table is assembled. Next, spread glue
on the contacting surfaces between one
of the side rails and its corresponding legs,
then fit the joints together, tapping them
into final position with a wooden mallet,
if required. Use two bar clamps to secure
the joints. Aligning the bars with the side
rail, lay the assembly on its side on a
work surface with one clamp under the
rail and one on top. Prop the tapered portion of the legs on wood blocks to keep
the assembly level. Protecting the stock
with wood pads, tighten the clamps evenly until a thin glue bead squeezes out of
the joints *(right)*. Repeat for the remaining
side rail and legs.

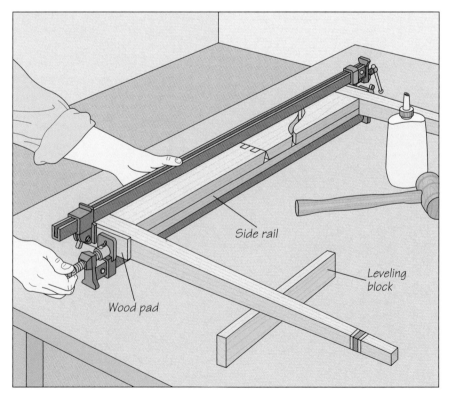

Side rail

Leveling
block

Wood pad

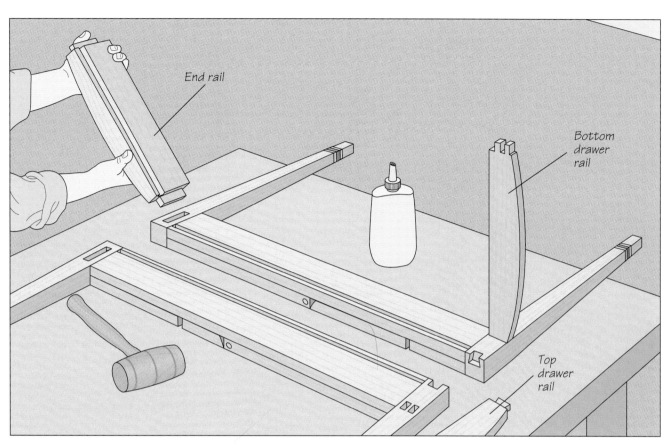

End rail

Bottom drawer rail

Top drawer rail

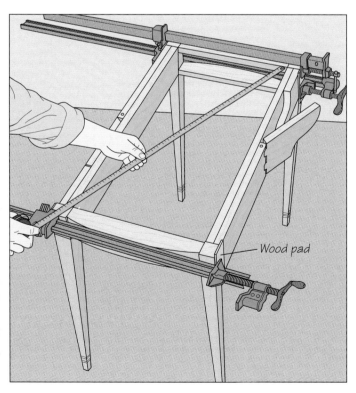

Wood pad

5 Gluing the end rail and drawer rails

Once the glue bonding the legs to the side rails has cured, remove the clamps and set the assemblies flat on a work surface with their mortises facing up. Test-fit and, if necessary, correct any ill-fitting joints and do any required sanding. Spread glue on the contacting surfaces between the end and drawer rails and the legs, then fit the bottom drawer rail and end rail into one of the side rail assemblies *(above)*. Position the other leg-and-rail assembly on top and set the framework upright on the floor. Finally, fit the top drawer rail into place and clamp the assembly *(step 6)*.

6 Installing the clamps

Use three bar clamps to secure the joints between the end and drawer rails and the legs. Protecting the stock with wood pads, install one clamp along the end rail and two more along the drawer rails. To check whether the assembly is square, measure the diagonals between opposite corners immediately after tightening the clamps *(left)*. They should be equal; if not, the assembly is out-of-square. To correct the problem, install a bar clamp across the longer of the two diagonals. Tighten this clamp a little at a time, measuring as you go until the two diagonals are equal.

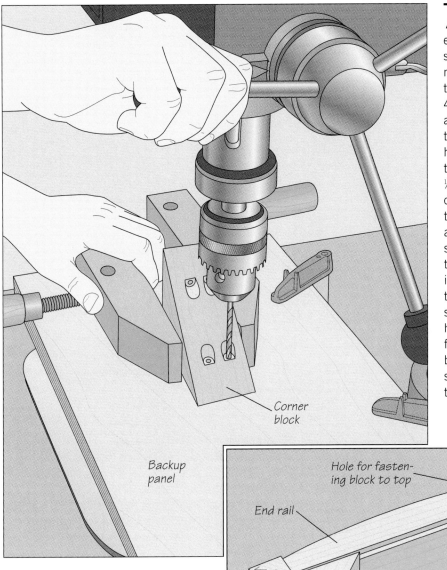

7 Making the corner blocks

Attach a triangular corner block to each joint between the end rail and the side rails; this will reinforce the back corners of the table and keep it square. To fit the blocks into the table corners, make a 45° miter cut at each end of the blocks and mark four points on the long edge, two near each end. Next, bore pocket holes through the blocks for the screws that will secure them to the rails. Install a ½-inch Forstner bit in your drill press and clamp a backup panel to the machine table. Secure the block in a handscrew and drill a shallow hole to recess the screw head. Reposition the block to bore the next hole, then turn the block around in the handscrew to drill the holes near the other end. Repeat the process with a smaller brad-point bit to bore clearance holes *(left)*. Finally, with the block top-face down on the table, drill a counter-bored hole through the middle of the surface; this hole will enable you to fasten to the block to the table top.

Corner block

Backup panel

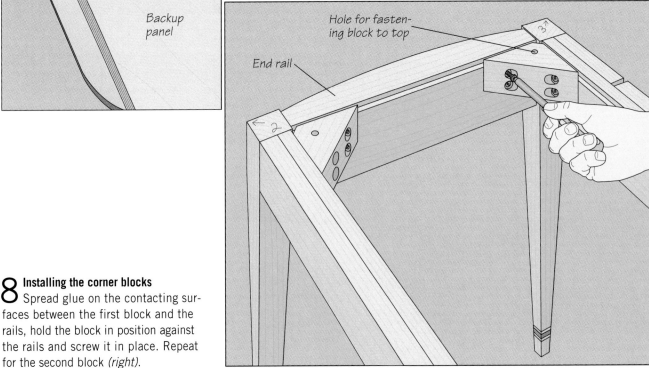

Hole for fastening block to top

End rail

8 Installing the corner blocks

Spread glue on the contacting surfaces between the first block and the rails, hold the block in position against the rails and screw it in place. Repeat for the second block *(right)*.

B uild the drawer for your Pembroke table as you would for a Queen Anne secretary, *(page 116)* using through dovetails to join the pieces. Use ¼-inch plywood for the drawer bottom. The Pembroke table drawer also gets a false front which is curved to match the shape of the end rail and drawer rails.

To install the drawer, start by fastening runners to the side rails, as shown below. Slide the drawer into its opening and clamp on the false front, then trace the curve of the top drawer rail onto the top edge of the false front *(page 42)* and cut the profile of the front. You can apply wax to the runners to help the drawer ride smoothly as it is opened and closed.

Supported by runners fastened to the side rails, the Pembroke table drawer shown above is assembled with through dovetails. The false front curves to match the profile of the end rail and drawer rails.

REINFORCING THE FRAME

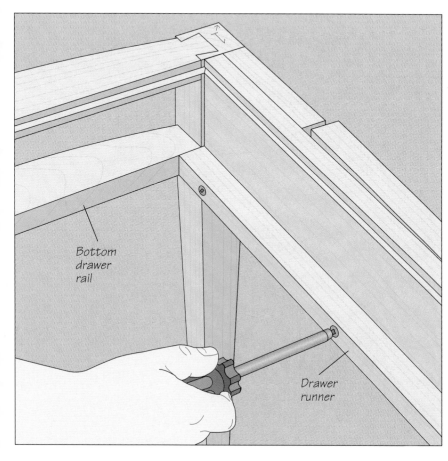

Bottom drawer rail

Drawer runner

1 Installing the drawer runners
Size the drawer runners, cutting them a few inches longer than the drawer. Drill three holes through the edges of each one, locating one hole near each end and one at the middle. Holding an edge of the runner against the side rail and one end against the bottom drawer rail, screw it in place *(left)*. The top face of the runner should be flush with the top face of the bottom drawer rail.

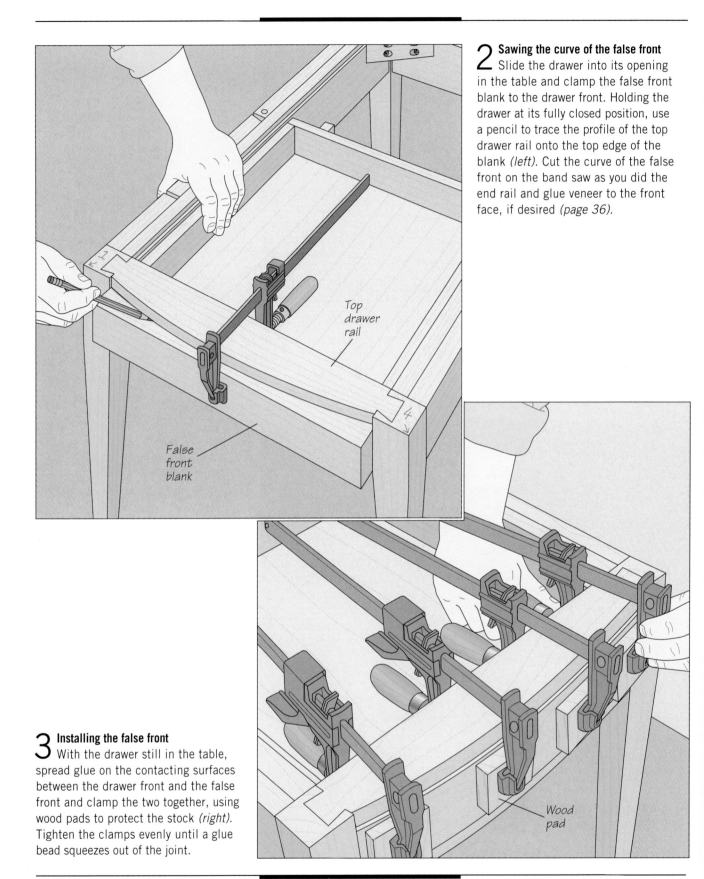

2 Sawing the curve of the false front
Slide the drawer into its opening in the table and clamp the false front blank to the drawer front. Holding the drawer at its fully closed position, use a pencil to trace the profile of the top drawer rail onto the top edge of the blank *(left)*. Cut the curve of the false front on the band saw as you did the end rail and glue veneer to the front face, if desired *(page 36)*.

Top
drawer
rail

False
front
blank

3 Installing the false front
With the drawer still in the table, spread glue on the contacting surfaces between the drawer front and the false front and clamp the two together, using wood pads to protect the stock *(right)*. Tighten the clamps evenly until a glue bead squeezes out of the joint.

Wood
pad

MAKING THE TOP

With the sides down, the top of the Pembroke table appears to be circular. Once the leaves are raised, however, the top's distinctive shape, with elliptical ends and sides, becomes apparent. Similar-shaped tabletops were used on Federal-period card tables. The leaves are hinged on a rule joint, which is shaped on the router table. Once the joint is completed and the hinges located, the curved profile of the leaves is cut on the band saw.

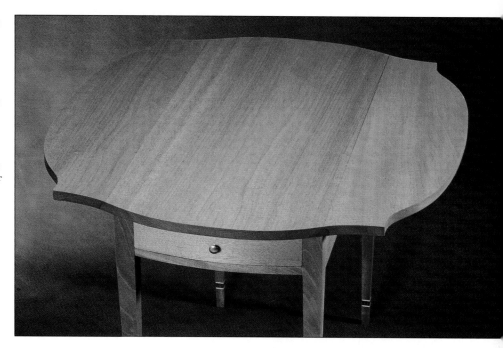

SHAPING THE TOP

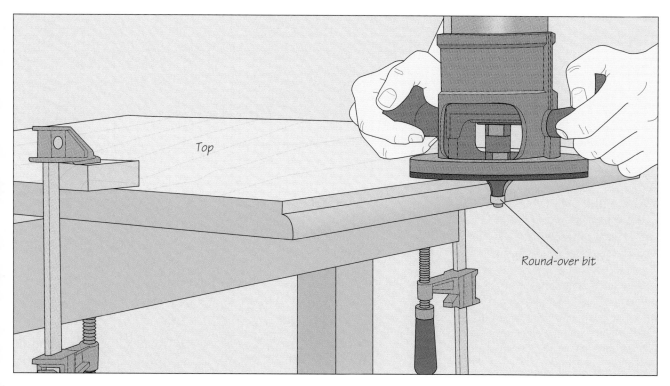

Top

Round-over bit

1 Routing the edges of the tabletop
Clamp the tabletop to a work surface with the edge to be shaped extending off the surface. Install a piloted round-over bit and adjust the cutting depth to allow you to reach the final depth in at least two passes. As you make the cut, press the bit pilot against the stock throughout the pass *(above)*. For a smooth finish, make your final pass a slow and shallow one.

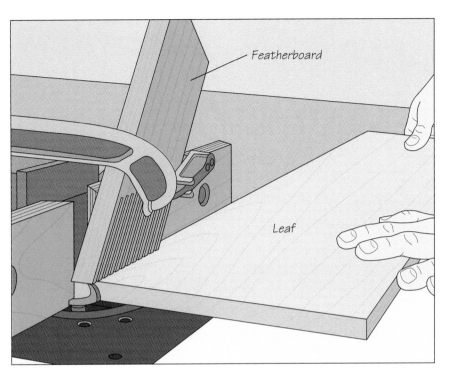

2 Routing the cove in the leaves
Install a piloted cove bit in the router and mount the tool in a table. Align the fence with the bit pilot bearing so the width of cut will equal one-half the cutter diameter. Clamp a featherboard to the fence on the infeed side of the bit to hold the workpiece flat against the router table. Set the depth of cut shallow to start; make several passes to reach your final depth gradually. Feed the leaf into the bit, pressing the edge of the work-piece firmly against the fence *(left)*. After each pass, test-fit the pieces until the top and the leaf mesh with a very slight gap between the two.

3 Attaching the leaves to the top
Join the leaves to the top by install-ing rule-joint hinges on the underside of the pieces. Set the top and leaves face down on a work surface, then mark lines along the shaped edges of the top in line with the start of each round-over cut, known as the fillet *(inset)*. Install three hinges for each leaf: one in the middle of the joint and one 5 inches from each end. With a paper shim inserted between the leaf and top, position a hinge leaf against the top and the other against the leaf at each hinge location so the pin is aligned with the fillet line, then outline the hinge. Chisel out the mortises, using a wider-blade tool to cut the mortises for hinge leaves and a narrower chisel to cut the slots for the pins *(right)*. Screw the hinges in place.

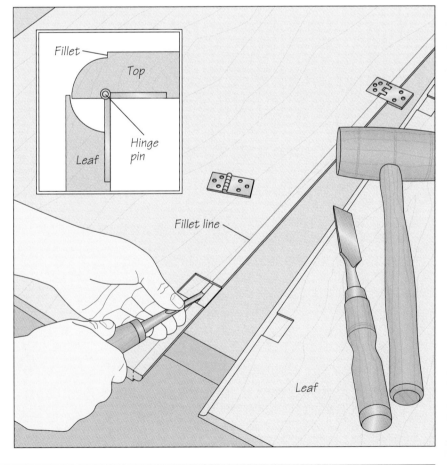

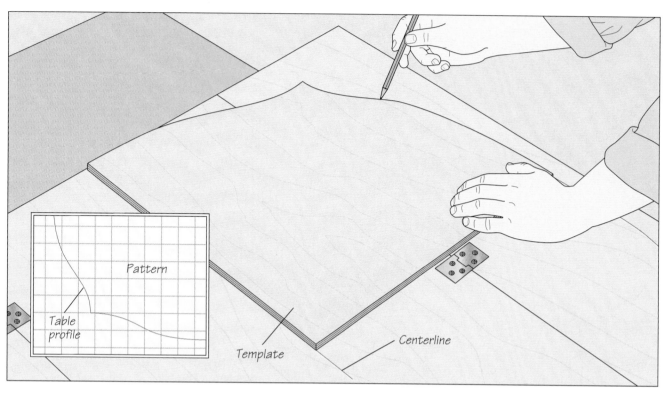

Pattern

Table profile

Template

Centerline

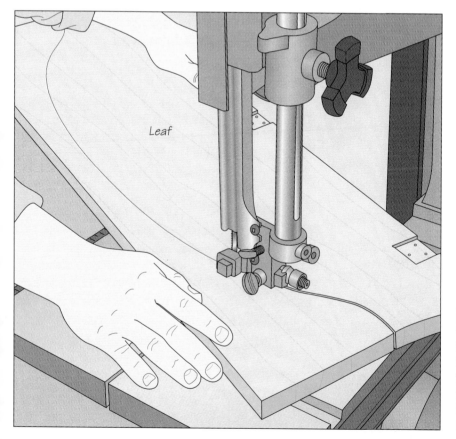

Leaf

4 Outlining the profile of the top

Enlarge the grid shown in the inset to produce a cutting pattern for shaping the profile of the top; one square equals 2 inches. Trace the pattern onto a piece of ¼-inch plywood or hardboard and cut out the template on your band saw. Then set the top face-down on a work surface and extend the leaves. Mark a line down the middle of the top and position the template on it; align the straight edge of the pattern with the centerline and the adjoining curved edge with the end of the top. Use a pencil to trace the curved profile on the top. Repeat at the remaining corners *(above)*.

5 Cutting the profile of the top

Unscrew the leaves from the top and use your band saw to cut the curved profile into each of the three pieces. Cut just to the waste side of your cutting line *(left)*, feeding the stock with both hands and keeping your fingers clear of the blade. Sand the cut edges to the line.

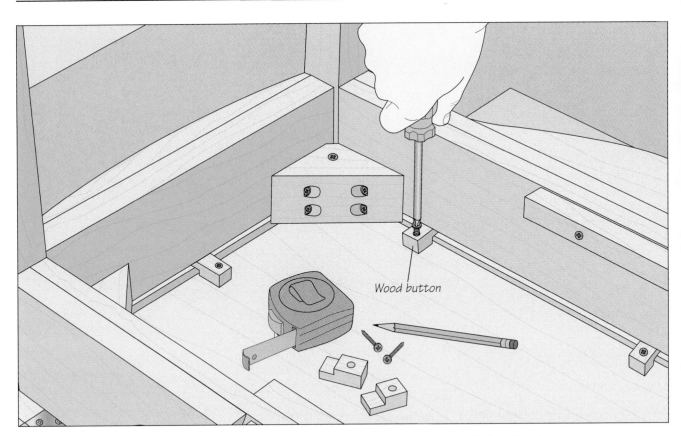

Wood button

SHOP TIP

Using steel tabletop fasteners
Commercial steel tabletop fasteners work like wood buttons: They are screwed to the top from underneath and grip a groove cut along the inside face of the rails. Because commercial fasteners are thinner than lipped wood buttons, the groove does not have to be cut with a dado blade (page 33); you can use a standard saw blade or a three-wing slotting cutter in a table-mounted router. To ensure proper tension, make the groove a little farther from the top than you would with the wood buttons.

6 Installing the top
The top is fastened to the table rails with wood buttons; screwed to the top, the buttons feature lips that fit into grooves cut into the rails (page 33), providing a secure connection while allowing for wood movement. Reinstall the rule-joint hinges in the top and leaves, and place the top face down on a work surface. Make a button for every 6 inches of rail length (page 133). Spacing them about 6 inches apart and leaving a ⅛-inch gap between the bottom of the grooves and the lipped ends of the buttons, screw the buttons in place (above). Once all the buttons are attached, drive a screw through each corner block into the top.

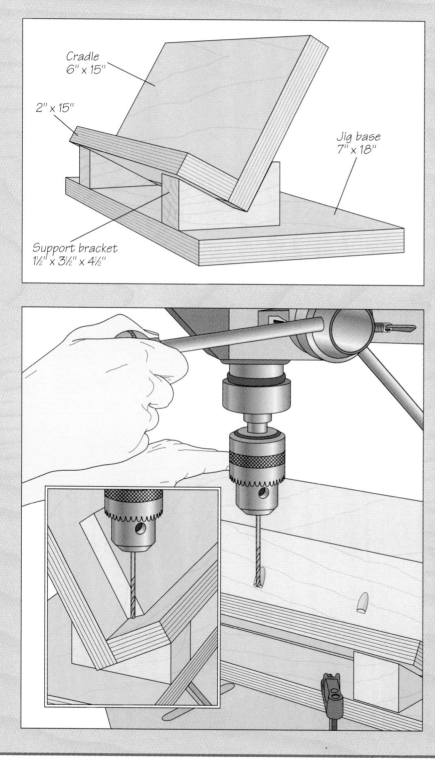

Cradle
6" x 15"

2" x 15"

Jig base
7" x 18"

Support bracket
1½" x 3½" x 4½"

POCKET-HOLE JIG

You can use pocket holes with screws as an alternative to wood buttons for attaching a tabletop to the side and end rails. The holes are drilled at an angle, and a pocket-hole jig *(left, top)*, shop-built from ¾-inch plywood, makes simple work of boring the holes on your drill press. For the jig, screw the two sides of the cradle together to form an L. Then cut a 90° wedge from each support bracket so that the wide side of the cradle will sit at an angle of about 15° from the vertical. Screw the brackets to the jig base and glue the cradle to the brackets.

To use the jig, seat a rail in the cradle with the side that will be drilled facing up. Drill the holes in two steps with two different bits: Use a Forstner bit twice the diameter of the screw heads for the entrance holes and a brad-point bit slightly larger than the diameter of the screw shanks for the exit holes. (The larger brad-point bit allows for wood expansion and contraction.)

To begin the process, install the brad-point bit and, with the drill press off, lower the bit with the feed lever, then position the jig and workpiece to center the bottom edge of the workpiece on the bit *(inset)*. Clamp the jig to the table and replace the brad-point bit with the Forstner bit.

Feed the bit slowly to drill the holes just deep enough to recess the screw heads. Then, install the brad-point bit and bore through the workpiece to complete the pocket holes *(left, bottom)*.

FOUR-POSTER BED

The four-poster bed is a dramatic and imposing piece of furniture that descends from the canopy beds of the Byzantine and medieval periods. Once, only heads of families could occupy a bed with a full canopy; others contented themselves with half-canopy beds, or unadorned beds.

The use of a canopied bed, then, was certainly a mark of status, but it also conveyed some practical benefits as well. The heavily quilted drapery that hung from the framework of boards called testers provided privacy, a rare commodity in a day when bedrooms served as family living and entertaining spaces. The folds of fabric also shut out the cold winter drafts that were common and, in summer, the drapes were replaced by light netting to keep insects at bay.

Status and utility aside, Americans have always simply liked the look of the four-poster. In its undraped form, the style has been an American favorite for almost 200 years.

The only real change in four-poster design occurred relatively recently, with the advent of box springs and spring mattresses. Before, a mattress was placed directly on a platform of rope stretched tightly between the bed rails. To resist the tension of the cords, the rails had to be quite stout—

Two sections of a bed post are being fitted together with a long mortise-and-tenon known as a tang joint. Located to coincide with decorative elements on the posts, the joints are virtually invisible. This one is not glued together, but assembled dry so the bed can be easily disassembled and transported.

as much as 3 inches thick. Box springs, however, could be laid on narrow cleats fastened to the inside of the rails, so the rails themselves could be reduced to a mere 1 inch thick, as they are today.

The most prominent feature of the bed are its four posts, each standing well over 6 feet tall. Given the 36-inch capacity of the typical lathe, turning the posts can seem to be an intimidating prospect. But, as shown on page 50, you can divide each post into four manageable segments and turn them separately. By introducing decorative elements like beads and coves adjacent to the joint lines the breaks are not noticeable and the posts appear to be solid turnings.

Like most beds, the one featured in this chapter has rails that are attached to the posts with knockdown hardware for quick disassembly. You can use bayonet brackets *(page 63)* that hook the rails onto the posts or bed bolts *(page 59)* to draw the rails and posts together by means of a bolt and tapped nut. Since the posts are glued to the headboard and footboard, all but one of the tang joints connecting the post segments together are left dry. This allows the posts to be taken apart without compromising the bed's structure. With the testers in place on the posts, the whole assembly is very rigid.

Whether they are graced by a canopy of hanging drapery or left bare, the uprights and testers of a four-poster bed are impressive. The mahogany bed shown at left also features a sunrise headboard.

ANATOMY OF A FOUR-POSTER BED

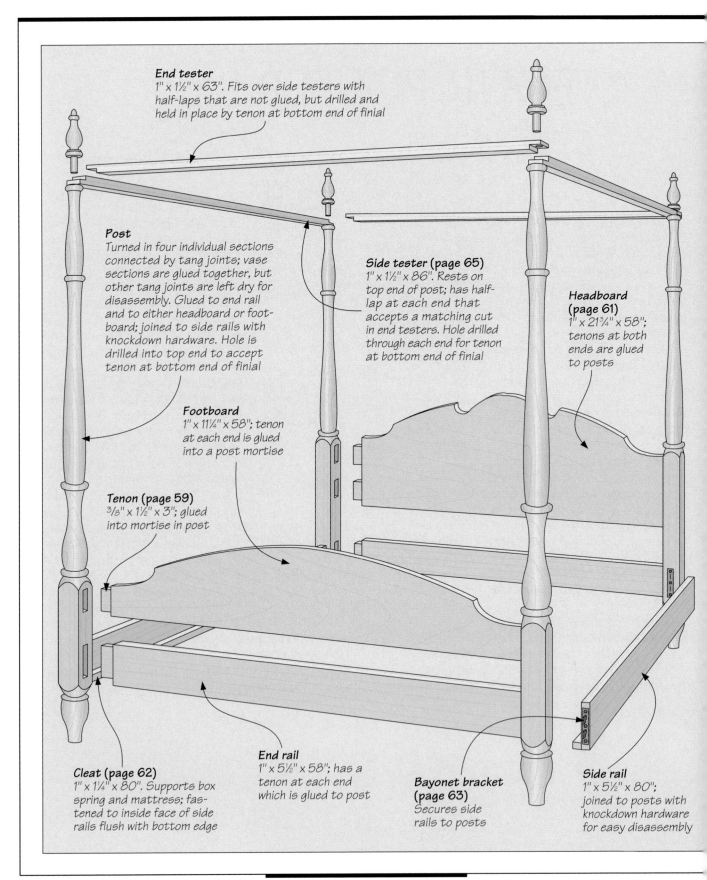

End tester
1" x 1½" x 63". Fits over side testers with half-laps that are not glued, but drilled and held in place by tenon at bottom end of finial

Post
Turned in four individual sections connected by tang joints; vase sections are glued together, but other tang joints are left dry for disassembly. Glued to end rail and to either headboard or footboard; joined to side rails with knockdown hardware. Hole is drilled into top end to accept tenon at bottom end of finial

Side tester (page 65)
1" x 1½" x 86". Rests on top end of post; has half-lap at each end that accepts a matching cut in end testers. Hole drilled through each end for tenon at bottom end of finial

Headboard (page 61)
1" x 21¾" x 58"; tenons at both ends are glued to posts

Footboard
1" x 11¼" x 58"; tenon at each end is glued into a post mortise

Tenon (page 59)
⅜" x 1½" x 3"; glued into mortise in post

Cleat (page 62)
1" x 1¼" x 80". Supports box spring and mattress; fastened to inside face of side rails flush with bottom edge

End rail
1" x 5½" x 58"; has a tenon at each end which is glued to post

Bayonet bracket (page 63)
Secures side rails to posts

Side rail
1" x 5½" x 80"; joined to posts with knockdown hardware for easy disassembly

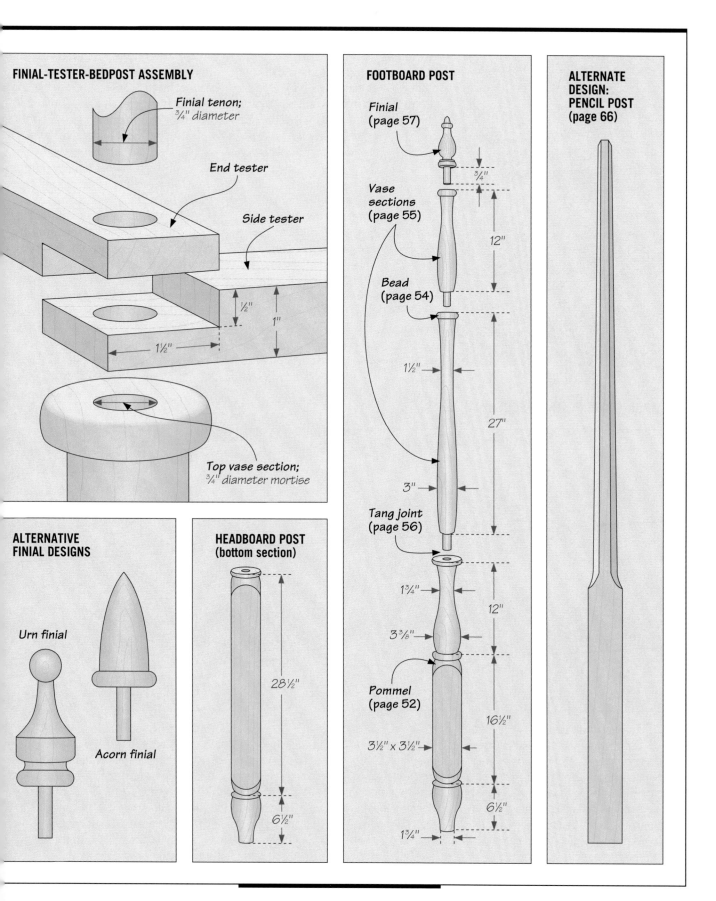

FINIAL-TESTER-BEDPOST ASSEMBLY

Finial tenon;
¾" diameter

End tester

Side tester

½"

1"

1½"

Top vase section;
¾" diameter mortise

ALTERNATIVE FINIAL DESIGNS

Urn finial

Acorn finial

HEADBOARD POST
(bottom section)

28½"

6½"

FOOTBOARD POST

Finial
(page 57)

¾"

Vase
sections
(page 55)

12"

Bead
(page 54)

1½"

27"

3"

Tang joint
(page 56)

1¾"

12"

3⅜"

Pommel
(page 52)

3½" x 3½"

16½"

6½"

1¾"

ALTERNATE DESIGN: PENCIL POST
(page 66)

TURNING THE BEDPOSTS

Turning the bedposts of a four-poster bed may appear to be a daunting challenge, but the project is manageable if broken down into its component parts. The design of the posts is simple; each one comprises only a few recurring elements, such as pommels, beads, vases,

The pommel, or bottom section, of a four-poster bedpost is turned with the help of a story pole and calipers. A story pole can serve as a shop-made turning guide. Cut from a strip of plywood, it includes key dimensions and diameters as well as the location of decorative elements like beads. A French curve is a good design tool for drawing on the pole. The calipers are used to check the size of the blanks as turning proceeds.

and tenons. See the anatomy illustrations on page 51 for details of the posts' diameters and the locations of the various elements. Each 6-foot-long post is turned in four individual sections, allowing for the 36-inch limit of most lathes. Since the sections are joined by tang joints, remember to allow for the 2-inch-long tenons when cutting your blanks to length.

Although the bottom sections of the footboard and headboard posts are different, the four posts are otherwise identical. To help keep them uniform, turn their matching sections one after another, rather than producing an entire post before moving on to the next one. Start with the bottom sections *(below)*, and move up, turning the vase sections *(page 55)* next and the finials *(page 57)* last.

MAKING THE POMMEL SECTIONS

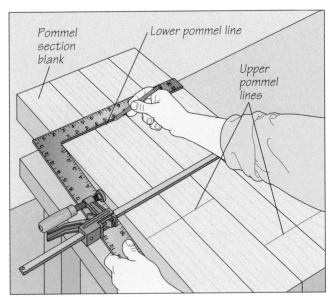

1 Defining the pommels
Cut the four pommel-section blanks to size, then outline the pommels—the transitions between the turned and square segments of the posts. Set the stock on a work surface and clamp the pieces together with their ends aligned so you can mark all the pommels at the same time. Although the upper pommels on the headboard posts are higher than on the footboard posts, the lower pommels are at the same height on all four pieces. Holding the edge of a carpenter's square against

the outside of the blanks, run a pencil along the arm to mark the lower pommels *(above, left)*. Mount one of the blanks between centers on your lathe and adjust the machine's speed to slow. Starting about ½ inch outside the lower pommel line, turn a V-groove into the corners of the blank with a skew chisel *(above, right)*. Deepen the groove until it runs completely around the workpiece. To avoid kickback, cut with the point of the blade with the bevel rubbing against the stock.

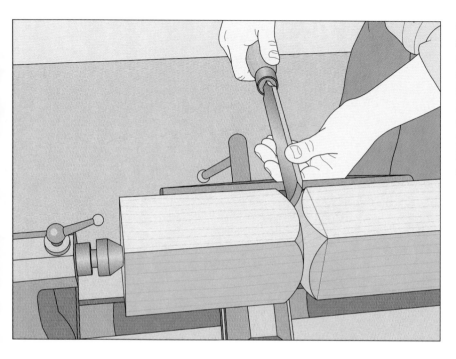

2 Shaping the pommel

Once you have finished the V-groove, widen it gradually, cutting with the long point of the chisel pointed forward. Roll the chisel from side to side while raising the handle so the bevel continues rubbing against the edges of the groove walls as you cut them *(left)*. Turn off the lathe after each cut to check the shape of the pommel.

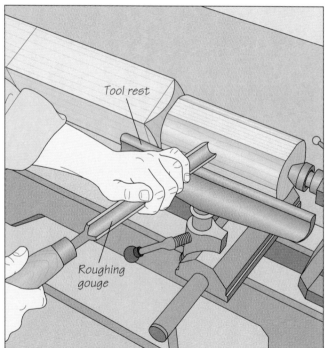

Tool rest

Roughing gouge

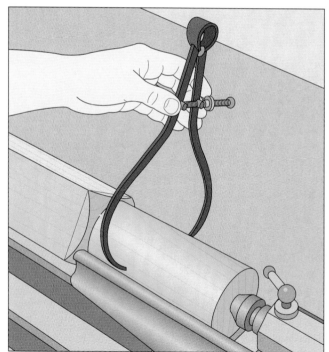

3 Turning the cylindrical part of the post

Once the pommel is finished, use a roughing-out gouge to turn the cylindrical portion of the post below the pommel. Holding the gouge with an overhand grip, brace it on the tool rest. Cut very lightly into the blank, making sure the bevel is rubbing against the stock and moving the gouge smoothly along the tool rest. As the gouge begins rounding the corners of the

post *(above, left)*, make successively deeper passes along the blank, raising the handle of the tool slightly with each pass, until the edges are completely rounded and you have a cylinder. Adjust the position of the tool rest as you progress to keep it close to the blank and periodically check the diameter of the bottom segment of the post with calipers *(above, right)*.

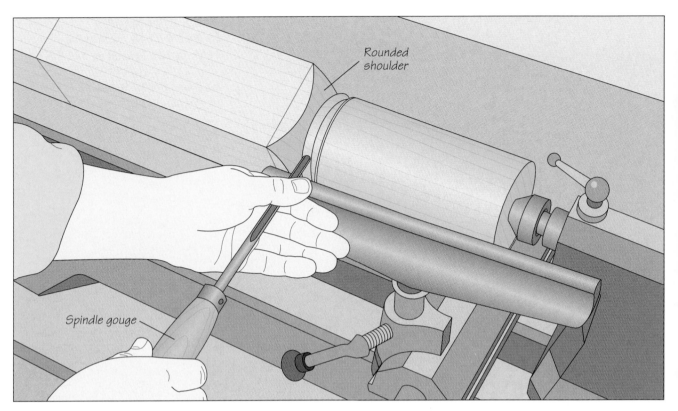

Rounded
shoulder

Spindle gouge

4 Turning the bead

Use a pencil to outline the bead between the lower pommel and cylindrical section of the post, then make a V-cut at each line with a skew chisel. Switch to a spindle gouge to finish the bead. Beginning at the center—or highest point—of the bead, hold the gouge flat and perpendicular to the post so its bevel is rubbing. Raise the handle and make a downhill cut—working from a high point to a low point—rotating the tool in the direction of the cut and angling the handle away *(above)*. The gouge should finish the cut resting on its side. Repeat for the other side of the bead, angling and rolling the tool in the opposite direction. Round the shoulders of the bead by blending it into the turning. Once the bead is finished, continue turning the bottom segment of the post until it has the shape shown on page 51. Repeat the process to turn beads at the upper pommel line and for both pommels of the remaining posts.

SHOP TIP

Using preset calipers
Since you are turning the various sections of the bedposts to different diameters, you can speed up the process by adjusting separate calipers for each feature of the blanks. For the turning shown at right, one pair is adjusted for the thicker part of the cylindrical segment, another is set for the bead below it, and a third is adjusted for the narrow section near the bottom of the workpiece. This will save you the trouble of continually readjusting a single pair of calipers. To avoid confusing the settings, attach a numbered strip of tape to each instrument.

TURNING THE VASE SECTIONS

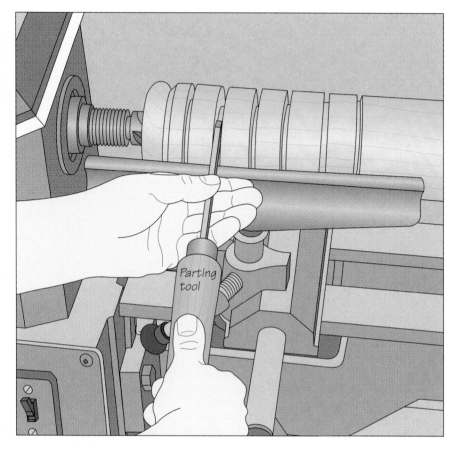

1 Making sizing cuts
Once the lower pommel sections of the four posts are done, turn to the vase sections. Each post has three vase segments: one at the top of the pommel section and two more above it. Although the bottommost one is the widest and the next one up is longest, the vases are otherwise identical and have similar contours. They also feature a tenon at the bottom end and a matching mortise at the top. To produce a vase, turn the segment into a cylinder *(page 53)*, then make a series of sizing cuts with a parting tool. Holding the parting tool with an underhand grip edge-up on the tool rest, raise the handle slightly so the blade cuts into the cylinder. Continue to raise the handle until the cut reaches the required depth *(left)*. Each cut should penetrate to the finished diameter of the post at that point; check your progress with calipers periodically. Twist the tool slightly from side to side as you make the cut to minimize friction and to prevent the blade from jamming.

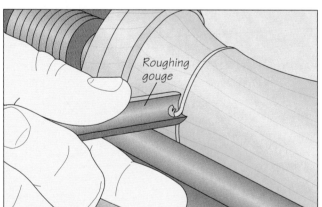

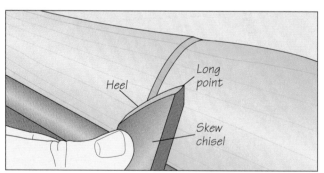

2 Roughing out the vase
Once you have finished all the sizing cuts, use a roughing gouge to clear out the waste between cuts. Follow the same procedure you would use to turn a cylinder, holding the tool with an overhand grip and always working in a downhill direction to avoid tearout *(above)*. Joining the sizing cuts will create a taper along the length of the workpiece. Use a spindle gouge to round over the ends of the vase.

3 Planing the vase smooth
Use a skew chisel to smooth the vase. Holding the tool with an underhand grip and with the lathe turned off, set the blade on the tool rest so that its long point is above the blank and its bevel is inclined in the direction of the cut; this is about 65° to the axis of the wood. Switch on the lathe and raise the handle slightly, bringing the cutting edge of the chisel into contact with the stock. Move the blade along the tool rest *(above)*, letting its bevel rub; do not allow the heel or long point dig into the wood. The center of the cutting edge should produce a series of thin shavings.

MAKING THE TANG JOINTS

1 Turning the tenons

Once you have turned all the vases, it is time to produce the tang joints. Start by turning tenons at the bottom ends of the two separate vase sections and finial blank. Mark the tenon shoulder 2 inches from the end of the workpiece by holding a pencil against the spinning blank. Then, holding a parting tool with an underhand grip, make a series of sizing cuts to define the tenon *(page 55)*. Use a roughing gouge to clear out the waste between the cuts. As the tenon begins to take shape, periodically check it with calipers, stopping when the tenon is ¾ inch in diameter. Finally, use a skew chisel to undercut the shoulder slightly; this will ensure that the bottom ends of the vase sections sit flush on the sections below without wobbling. Hold the chisel edge-up so its long point and bevel are aligned with the shoulder line. Then slowly raise and twist the handle, slicing deeper into the shoulder as the cutting edge approaches the tenon *(right)*.

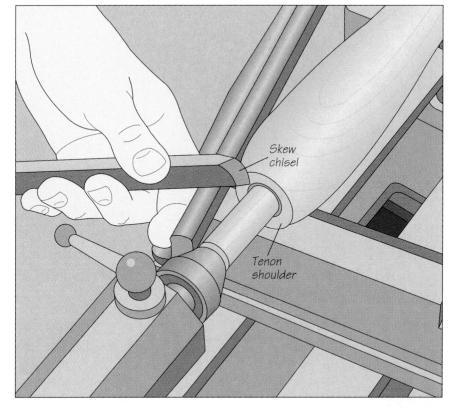

2 Boring the mortises

Remove the blank and tool rest, and adjust the lathe to its slowest speed. Mount a ¾-inch drill bit in a Jacobs chuck and attach the chuck to the lathe tailstock. Mount the tenon-end of the blank in the headstock and slide the tailstock along the bed until the bit meets the center of the workpiece. Then turn on the lathe and turn the handwheel to advance the tailstock so the bit bores straight into the end of the blank *(above)*; be sure to hold the workpiece steady at the start of the operation.

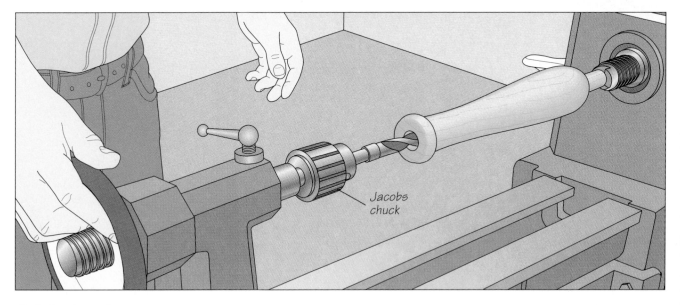

TURNING THE FINIALS

1 Shaping the finials
The finials at the top of the bedposts combine vases and beads. After turning these elements, separate the top end of the finial from the waste wood used to hold the blank between centers. To avoid marring the finial's rounded top, use a skew chisel to part off the workpiece. Holding the tool with an underhand grip, make a slicing cut with the long point of the blade as you would round a pommel *(page 53)*. Make a series of deeper V-cuts *(right)*. Before the finished turning breaks loose from the waste, support it with one free hand, keeping your fingers well clear of the tool rest and being careful not to grip the spinning workpiece.

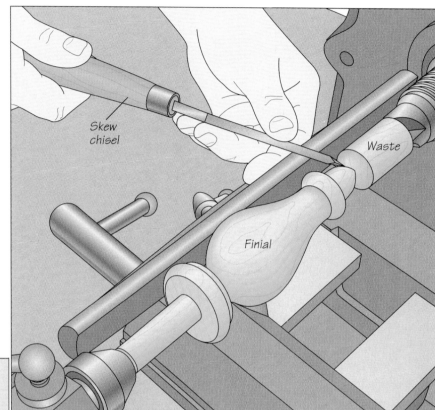

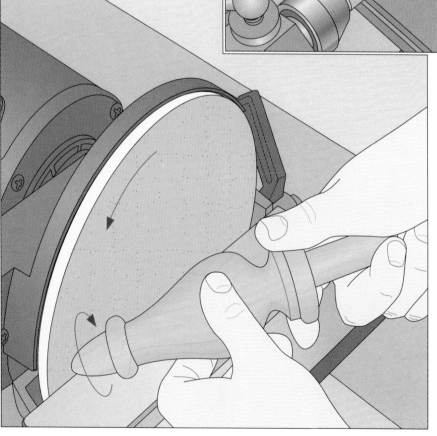

2 Smoothing the finial
To remove any tool marks left on the finials by the skew chisel, sand their surfaces smooth. You can do the job by hand, securing the stock in a bench vise and using a sanding block. But a disk sander like the one shown at left will make quick work of the task. Holding the finial on the sanding table, ease it into the disk at an angle of about 45°. Applying light pressure, rotate the finial until it is smooth.

PREPARING THE POSTS FOR THE END BOARDS AND RAILS

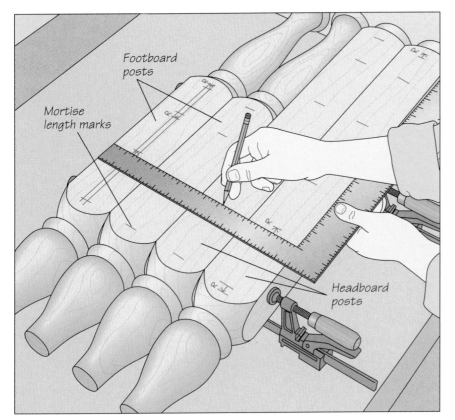

Footboard posts

Mortise length marks

Headboard posts

1 Laying out the mortises
The bedposts are joined to the end boards and rails with blind mortise-and-tenons. To ensure that all the mortises line up, mark them on the posts in a single setup. Clamp the posts together with their ends aligned and place the assembly on a work surface. Holding the edge of a carpenter's square against the stock, mark on one post at a time. Mark the mortise length—3 inches—across the pommel; each headboard post has three mortises, including two for the headboard and one for the end rail, while each footboard post has two—one for the footboard and one for the rail. Next, mark the mortise width—⅜ inch; center the mortise outline on the pommels. Use the square to align all the mortise length marks *(left)*.

2 Drilling the mortises
You can cut the mortises in the posts by hand with a chisel and mallet, or use a router fitted with a mortising bit. But considering the depth of the mortises—1⅝ inches—a hollow chisel mortiser, like the one shown at right or a drill press with a mortising attachment, will do the job most quickly and accurately. Set up the machine following the manufacturer's directions. For the mortiser shown, install a ⅜-inch bit and place one of the posts on the table, centering a mortise outline under the cutter. Butt the fence against the stock and adjust the hold-down to secure the post while still allowing you to slide the workpiece freely along the fence. Make a cut at each end of the outline, then a series of staggered cuts in between *(right)* to complete the mortise.

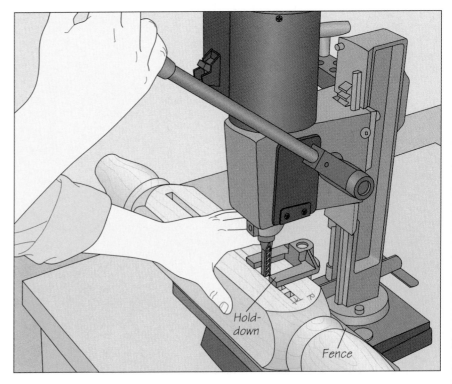

Hold-down

Fence

MAKING THE END BOARDS

The sunrise motif of the headboard featured in this chapter is a popular design, particularly in American Country furniture. Whatever design you choose, however, the primary challenge in making the end boards for a bed is cutting the pieces symmetrically. The boards are too unwieldy to do the job accurately on the band saw. You will be much better off shaping the boards with a router guided by templates, as shown starting on page 61.

When the time comes to glue the end boards and rails to the bedposts (page 64), try to enlist the aid of an assistant or two to help you maneuver the stock and the six long bar clamps you will need. For maximum flexibility at glue-up, use white glue rather than yellow adhesive; it takes longer to set, allowing more time for adjustment after it has been applied.

Join the side rails to the posts with commercial bayonet brackets (page 63) or bed bolts (photo, right). Bed bolts are stronger, but the brackets are simpler to install and come apart with only a few mallet taps.

To facilitate disassembly, bedposts are usually attached to the side rails with knockdown hardware, such as the bed bolt shown at right. The bolt extends through the post into the rail and is threaded into a cross dowel installed in the rail. The bolt head is concealed by an embossed brass cover.

CUTTING THE TENONS

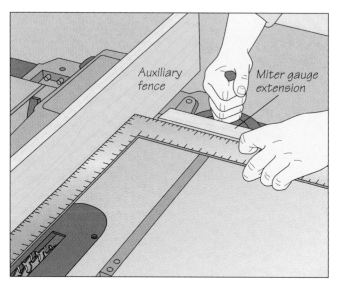

Auxiliary fence

Miter gauge extension

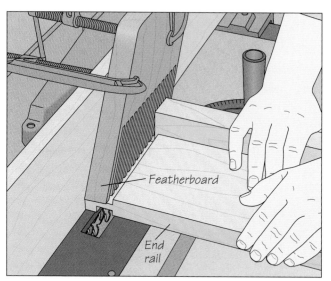

Featherboard

End rail

1 Sawing the tenon cheeks

You can cut the tenon cheeks in the end boards and rails with a router or a radial arm saw. If you do the job on a table saw, as shown here, you will need to set up an auxiliary table or work with a helper to keep the long workpieces steady as you feed them across the table. Start by installing a dado head on the saw, adjusting it to its widest setting. Attach a high auxiliary fence and an extension board to the miter gauge. Hold a carpenter's square against the fence and extension to ensure that they are perpendicular to each other and adjust the miter gauge, if necessary (above, left). Set the cutting height at about ¼ inch and make a cut across each face of a scrap board as thick as the end boards and rails. Test-fit the tenon in one of the post mortises, raising the dado head and making additional cuts, as necessary, until the fit is snug. Once the blade height is set, position the fence for a 1½-inch-wide cut and clamp a featherboard to the fence above the dado head. Holding the workpiece flush against the fence and miter gauge extension, and flat on the table, feed it into the blades to define the tenon shoulder. Then shift the stock away from the fence by the width of the kerf and make another pass to clear the remaining waste. Turn the workpiece over to cut the cheek on the other side (above, right).

2 Marking the edges of the tenons

Once all the tenon cheeks have been cut, mark the tenons' edges, using their post mortises as a guide. Outline single tenons on the end rails and footboard; the headboard, shown at right, has two tenons. Set the post on a work surface with its mortises facing up and position the mating piece on top, aligning the end of the board with the mortises. Then line up the blade of a combination square with one end of a mortise and, holding the handle of the square against the end of the tenon and the tip of the blade against the shoulder, mark the tenon edge across the cheek with a pencil. Outline the remaining tenon edges the same way *(right)*, marking the waste with Xs as you go.

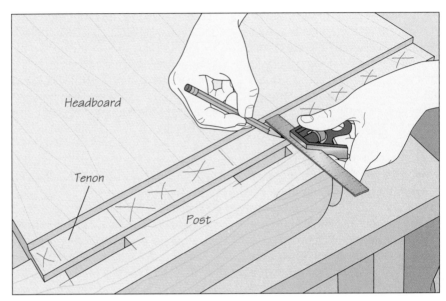

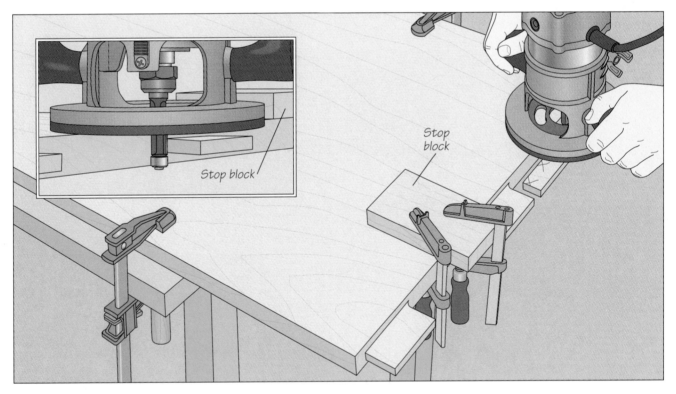

3 Finishing the tenons

Clear the waste adjoining the edges of the tenons using a router fitted with a bottom-piloted flush-trimming bit. Clamp the stock to a work surface and align the cutter with the edge of a tenon. Then butt a stop block against the router base plate and clamp it to the workpiece. If there is a second tenon on the same end of the stock, as in the headboard, clamp a second stop block to prevent the router from cutting into the tenon.

With the tool's base plate flat on the workpiece and flush against the stop block, ease the bit into the stock until the pilot bearing reaches the tenon shoulder. Feed the router along the end of the board, stopping when the base plate contacts a second stop block *(inset)* or the bit reaches the edge of the workpiece *(above)*. Clean up the edges of the tenon with a chisel.

SHAPING THE END BOARDS

1 Making the end board templates
Shape the curved profiles of the head- and footboards with a router guided by templates. Make the templates from ¾-inch plywood, tracing the contours of the boards' top edges, as illustrated on page 51, on the plywood. But instead of producing templates that span the full end boards, mark only one-half the patterns on the templates, from one end to the middle; not only will the templates be easier to maneuver, but by using a single pattern to outline both halves of each board, you will ensure that they are symmetrical. Cut each pattern one-half as long as the end board, plus about 12 inches. On both sides of the template, mark one end of the end board, then the middle, and trace the curved pattern in between. Cut the pattern on your band saw, then smooth the cut edge, using a spindle sander *(right)* or a sanding block.

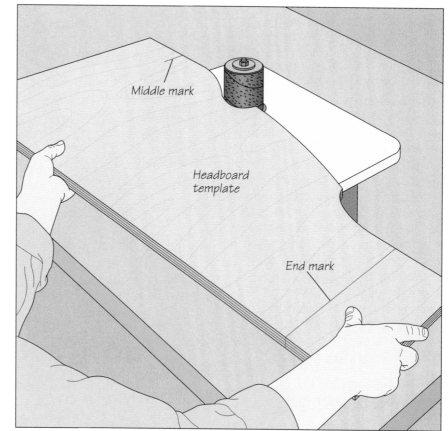

Middle mark

Headboard template

End mark

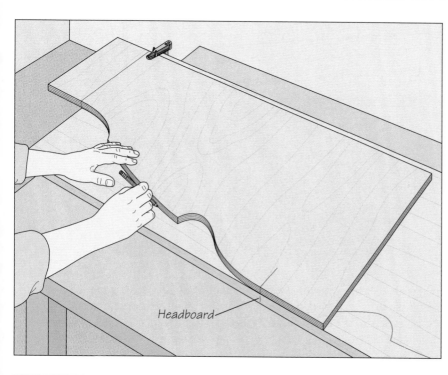

Headboard

2 Marking the end board stock
Set the stock face-up on a work surface and mark the middle on the top edge. Then clamp the template on top, aligning the end mark with the end of the workpiece and the two middle marks. Run a pencil along the cut edge of the template to outline the pattern on the end board stock *(left)*. Then turn the template over and repeat the process to mark the other half of the workpiece.

3 Shaping the end boards

Cut the end boards on your band saw, leaving about ⅛ inch of waste along the cutting lines. Reclamp the workpiece and template to a work surface as in step 2, ensuring that the edge to be shaped extends off the table by a few inches. Install a top-piloted flush-trimming bit in your router, adjusting the cutting depth so the pilot bearing will be level with the template and the cutter will trim the entire edge of the stock. Starting at one end of the board, hold the router flat on the template and ease the bit into the stock until the bearing contacts the pattern. Then feed the tool steadily along the edge, moving against the direction of bit rotation and pressing the bearing against the template *(right)*. Once you reach the end of the template, stop the cut. Turn the template over and clamp it to the other half of the end board, then repeat the trimming process. Smooth the edges of the stock with 120-grit sandpaper.

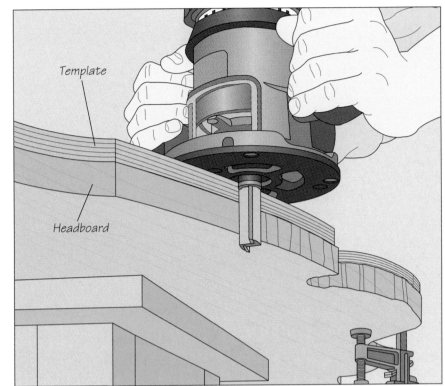

Template

Headboard

PREPARING THE SIDE RAILS

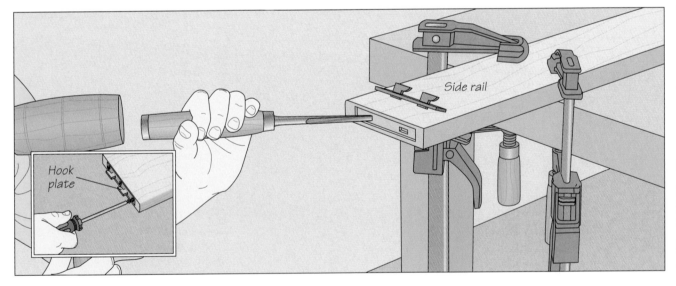

Side rail

Hook plate

1 Fastening hook plates to the rails

If you are using bayonet brackets to attach the side rails to the posts, start by fixing a hook plate to the ends of the rails. Clamp a rail to a work surface, center a plate on the end, and outline it with a pencil. Then chisel a mortise within the outline to a depth equal to the plate thickness. Once the plate is flush with the end of the rail, hold it in position and tap it with a mallet to mark the base of the hooks on the wood. Hold the chisel perpendicular to the end grain of the rail and cut recesses for the hooks *(above)*. Then screw the plate to the rail, making sure that the hooks will be pointing down.

2 Fastening catch plates to the posts

The placement of the catch plates on the bedposts determines the height of the mattress; the bottom of the box spring is customarily 8$\frac{1}{2}$ inches above the floor. It is also crucial to locate the plates so the inside faces of the rails hug the edges of the box spring; for a 60-inch-wide box spring/mattress set in a bed of the dimensions provided on page 50, centre the plate on the edge of the post. Mark the edges of the rail on the post and outline the catch plate on the post *(right)*, centering it between rail marks. Chisel the plate mortise as you did in step 2, then hold the hardware in position and outline the hook openings on the stock. Use a chisel and mallet to cut recesses in the post for the hooks, then screw the catch plate to the post.

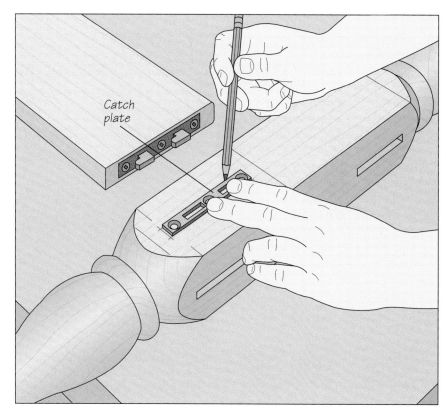

Catch plate

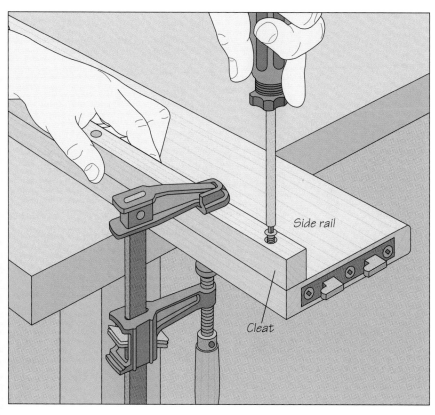

Side rail

Cleat

3 Fastening the cleats to the side rails

Once all the bayonet brackets are installed, cut the cleats that will support the box spring to the length of the side rails. Spread glue on the contacting surfaces between the side rail and cleat, then clamp the cleat along the inside face of the rail, flush with the bottom edge; make sure the ends of the two pieces are aligned. Next, drill pilot holes through the cleat and into the rail, starting 2 inches in from the ends and spacing the remaining holes 8 inches apart. Finally, drive a screw into each hole *(left)*.

GLUING UP THE BEDPOSTS AND END BOARDS

1 Gluing the bedpost vase sections together

Although the joints connecting the pommel sections and finials of the posts to the vase sections are not glued, the tang joints between the vase sections must be glued to give the posts adequate rigidity. Spread adhesive on the tenon and in the mortise of the tang joint and on the contacting surfaces between the two pieces, then secure them in a bar clamp, protecting the stock with wood pads. If the post begins to distort as you tighten the clamp, reposition it in the jaws until it remains straight. Keep tightening *(right)* until a glue bead squeezes out of the joint.

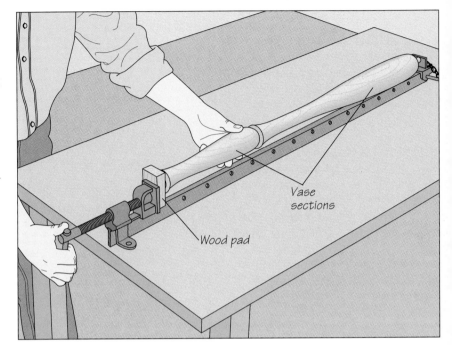

Vase sections

Wood pad

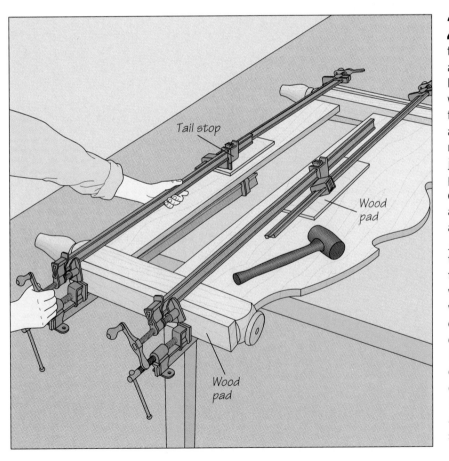

Tail stop

Wood pad

Wood pad

2 Gluing the posts to the end boards

Set the end boards with their respective end rails and posts on a work surface, and test-fit the mortise-and-tenon joints between them. Use a chisel to pare away wood from any ill-fitting joints. Apply glue to the contacting surfaces of the posts and end boards and rails, and use a non-marring dead-blow hammer to tap the joints together, if necessary. Secure the pieces with four long pipe clamps or eight shorter bar clamps used in pairs, as shown at left. Position two clamps across the end board so the handle-end jaws rest against opposite posts and the tail stops of the clamps overlap. Protect the posts with wood pads cut as long and wide as the pommel sections; use plywood pads to protect the faces of the end boards and rails. Tighten one of the clamps until the tail stops make contact. Repeat with two more clamps across the end rail and partially tighten all four clamps, then turn the assembly over and install the remaining four clamps. Tighten all the clamps *(left)* until a thin glue bead squeezes out of the joints.

MAKING AND INSTALLING THE TESTERS

1 Notching the ends of the testers

Once the bedposts, end boards, and rails are glued up and assembled, it is time to prepare the testers that connect the top ends of the posts. Use your table saw to cut the half-laps that join the testers. Install a dado head, adjusting it to its maximum width, and set the cutting height at one-half the stock thickness. Screw an extension board to the miter gauge. Position the rip fence for a width of cut equal to the width of the testers, then cut each half-lap in two passes. Start by aligning the end of the board with the dado head and, holding the edge of the tester flush against the miter gauge extension, feed the stock into the cut. Make the second pass the same way, but with the end of the board flush against the fence *(right)*.

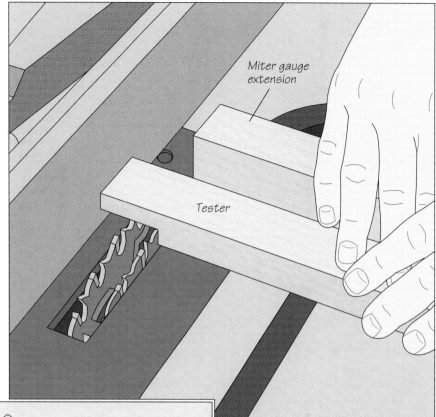

Miter gauge extension

Tester

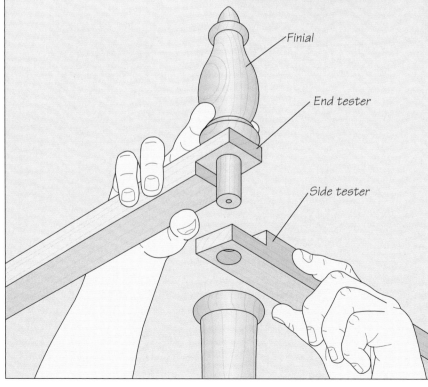

Finial

End tester

Side tester

2 Installing the testers

Bore a hole through the center of each half-lap at the end of the testers, using your drill press fitted with a bit the same diameter as the finial tenons—¾ inch. To prevent tearout, bore the holes in two steps: Start by drilling halfway through the stock, then turn the tester over and complete the hole from the other side. (You can also assemble the testers and drill the two holes at the same time with a portable drill. This will ensure that the holes line up perfectly.) Install the testers at one corner of the bed at a time. Slip the finial tenon through the hole in the end tester and, holding the side tester over the bedpost *(left)*, fit the tenon through its hole into the mortise in the post.

PENCIL POSTS

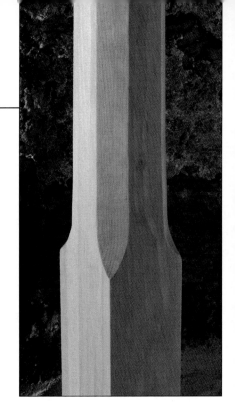

The tapered octagonal bedpost, known as a pencil post, is a popular alternative to the turned version featured in the previous section. Instead of being shaped in individual sections that are then assembled, pencil posts are made from a single length of solid or face-glued lumber—first tapered on a jointer *(page 67)* and then by hand *(page 68)*. To avoid tearout as you shape the posts, make your blanks from 3½-inch-thick stock with straight grain; if you choose to glue up thinner boards to make up the blanks, make sure the wood grain of the pieces runs in the same direction.

Shaping the octagonal sections of the posts is a challenge of design and execution. The bevels that create the octagon must be laid out so the eight sides are equal as the post tapers from base to tip. Although the layout method shown below is straightforward, it demands precise drafting.

With its solid, square base giving way to an octagonal section that gradually tapers to a narrow tip, the pencil post shown at right offers both strength and refinement. The curved bevels that mark the transition between the square and octagonal segments are known as lamb's tongues.

MAKING PENCIL POSTS

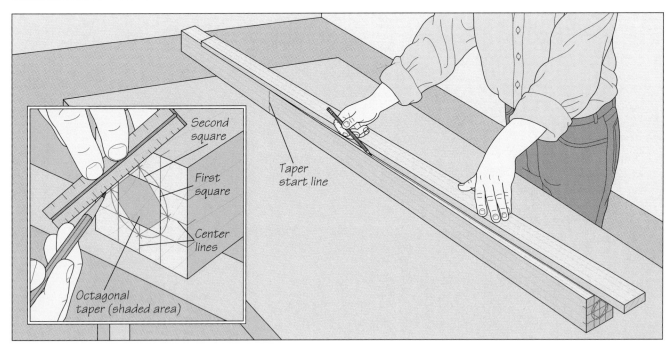

Second square

First square

Center lines

Octagonal taper (shaded area)

Taper start line

1 Outlining the tapers

For a bed of the dimensions shown on page 50, mark a line for the start of the taper all around the blank 20 inches from the bottom end. Then outline the octagonal taper on the center of the top end. Start by centering a 1¼-inch square on the end with sides parallel to the stock's side. Extend the sides of the square to the edges of the stock, then draw vertical and horizontal lines through the center, each bisecting the square's sides. Next use a compass to draw a circle from the center of the square that passes through each of its four corners. Then, with a pencil and ruler, draw a second square whose corners meet where the circle and center lines intersect *(inset)*. The octagonal shape will be cut by first tapering the stock to the dimensions of the first square you drew, then by planing the corners of that square down to the remaining sides of the second square. Mark the first cuts by using a pencil and long straightedge to extend the taper lines from the end to the start line *(above)*.

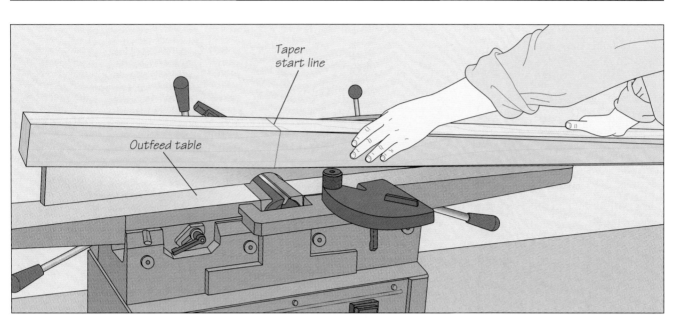

2 Setting up and starting the taper

An easy way to taper the posts is with a jointer. Set the machine for a shallow cut and position the fence to expose only about 4 inches of the cutterhead. For this operation, also adjust the guard out of the way. Then, holding the blank against the fence, align the taper start line with the front of the outfeed table. To start each pass, carefully lower the blank onto the cutterhead while holding it firmly against the fence *(above)*. Make sure both hands are over the infeed side of the table.

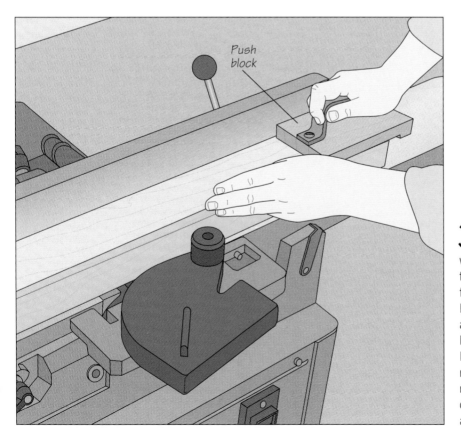

3 Tapering the posts

Feed the leg across the cutterhead with a push block, pressing down on the trailing end of the stock while holding it flush against the fence *(left)*. Keep your left hand away from the cutterhead. Make as many passes as necessary until you have trimmed the stock to the taper outline, repeating the process to shape the remaining faces. If your markings are correct, you should make the same number of passes on each side. Clean up the taper at the start line using a belt sander.

BEVELING TAPERS

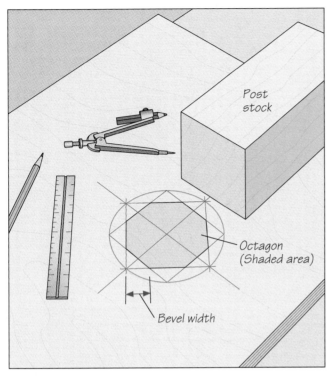

Post stock

Octagon (Shaded area)

Bevel width

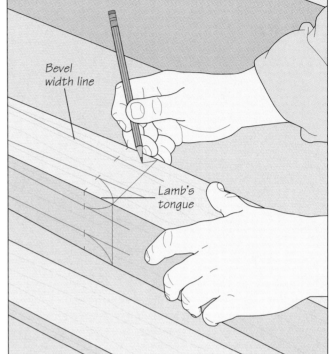

Bevel width line

Lamb's tongue

1 Laying out the bevels

To form the octagon, bevel the corners of the square taper. The bevel is already outlined on the end of each post, but it must also be marked on the sides of the stock. Taking the dimensions from a piece of full-size post stock, and drawing on scrap plywood, outline squares as you did in step 1 *(above, left)*. Transfer your measurement—equal to the bevel width—to the post, measuring from each corner of the square to either side. Then use a pencil and a long straightedge to connect each mark with its corresponding point on the octagon drawn at the top end of each post. Once all eight bevel lines are marked, draw a curved lamb's tongue at each corner, joining the bevel marks with the taper start line *(above, right)*.

2 Roughing out the bevels

To secure the posts, use three wood blocks. Cut V-shaped notches into an edge of each one, then place two of the blocks under the workpiece to support it and clamp one on top between the other two; position two of the blocks around the square portion of the post. Then use a drawknife to shape the tapered portion of the posts into octagons, beveling one corner at a time. Holding the drawknife on the stock bevel-side down, pull the tool toward the top end of the post *(right)*. The depth of cut depends on how much you tilt the handles; the lower the angle, the shallower the cut. Take a light shaving, always following the wood grain.

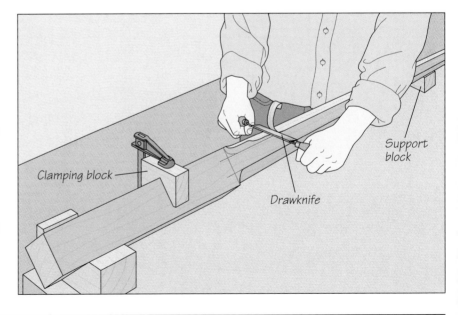

Clamping block

Drawknife

Support block

3 Smoothing the bevels

Once all the bevels have been cut, use a bench plane to flatten the eight sides of the posts' tapered section. Adjust the tool to a very light cut and work from the taper start line toward the post's top end to level the surface *(right)*. To avoid tearout, work with the wood grain. Reposition the post in the wood blocks as necessary to flatten the remaining sides.

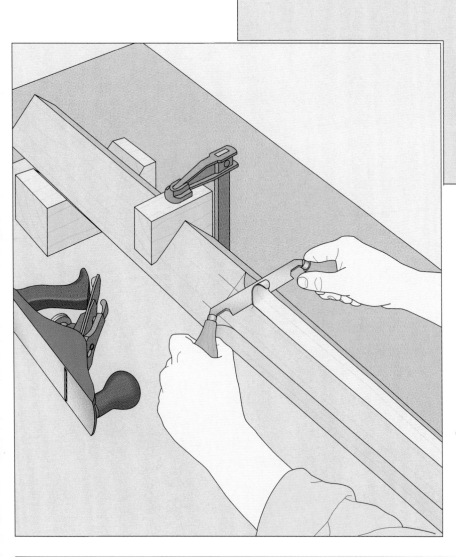

4 Shaping the lamb's tongue

To complete the pencil posts, switch back to the drawknife bring the lamb's tongues to their final shape. Work as you did in step 5, smoothing out the transition between the tongues and the bevel lines *(left)*. Once you are finished draw-knifing, smooth the surface using a sanding block.

WINDSOR CHAIR

The Windsor chair is a study in contrasts. Originally designed as an artless furnishing, it is now considered to be a sophisticated example of modern chair making. The simple elements of a Windsor—the sculpted seat and the hand-shaped legs, stretchers, arm posts, and spindles—belie the precise engineering required to assemble it. And despite its relatively lightweight components, the Windsor chair is very strong and durable.

First made in rural southern England, Windsor chairs came to North America in the mid-18th Century. Perhaps as a result of its practical design and unsophisticated construction, the style quickly flourished with America's pioneer homesteaders. The foundation of all Windsor chairs—whether the sack-back version featured in this chapter, the comb-back with its high backrest, or the continuous-arm type—is the solid-wood seat. Traditionally cut from a "green" (or freshly felled) log, the Windsor's seat represented an important innovation in chair making. In earlier styles, the back of the chair was an extension of the legs. This meant that the rear legs had to be bent to provide comfortable seating and were attached to the seat frame with relatively complex joinery.

The legs of a Windsor chair are not bent. Instead, the back and leg assemblies are independent, anchored separately to

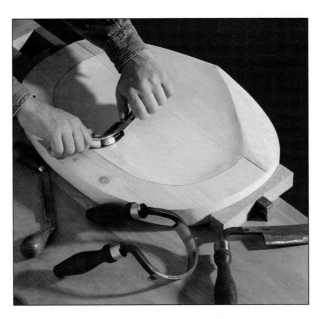

The top of a Windsor chair seat is traditionally sculpted by hand. With shaping tools like the spokeshave, inshave, and drawknife, it is possible to customize the seat for its user.

the seat at whatever angles suit its user. All of the chair's parts are joined with round mortise-and-tenons—a fairly simple joint to produce. Some woodworkers contend that one of the benefits of making a Windsor chair with green lumber is that you can take advantage of the hygroscopic, or moisture-absorbing character of wood. By drying the leg tenons prior to assembly and fitting them into "wet" mortises in the seat, a snug joint will become even tighter. Once the joint is assembled, the tenon will absorb moisture from the wood surrounding the mortise, swelling the tenon and shrinking the mortise. Other chair makers choose instead to use seasoned wood for the seat, which will be less likely to crack as it dries, and reinforce the joinery in other ways. The joints in the chair featured in this chapter are glued and many of them—such as the leg-to-seat joints—are further strengthened by wedges inserted in kerfs cut in the end of the tenons.

A final advantage of building a Windsor chair is that the entire process can be done with hand tools. Although the legs and stretchers can be turned on a lathe *(page 89)*, they can also be shaped—along with the spindles—using a drawknife *(page 76)* and a shop-built shaving horse *(page 78)*. The seat can be cut with a bowsaw *(page 84)*, then shaved and adzed to its finished shape.

The sack-back Windsor chair shown at left was finished with milk paint, a traditional finish for American Country furniture. Available in powdered form and mixed with water to a paint-like consistency, milk paint reflects the simplicity of the Windsor chair; it is best applied by brush.

Many of the round mortise-and-tenon joints that hold a Windsor chair together are reinforced by wedges. As the illustration at right shows, the top end of the legs, arm posts, and spindles are all kerfed prior to assembly; the wedges that fill the kerfs expand the tenons, ensuring that they fit snugly in their mortises.

But a Windsor chair is more than the sum of its parts. For strength and comfort, it also relies on the interaction of its various assemblies. The legs and stretchers, for example, work against each other to support the weight of its user. The back assembly, with its bow, arm, and spindles, functions in a similar manner. The legs splay out to the sides and are raked forward and backward—providing a broad, stable base for the chair. As with all enduring designs the seat is tilted back slightly, making the chair more comfortable.

The three views of the sack-back Windsor presented on page 73 provide you with the critical angles, spacings, and dimensions. More dimensions appear in the cutting list below and throughout the chapter where each part of the chair is made.

As you prepare your stock, keep in mind that you will not be able to cut some of the parts to their finished length until you begin final assembly. The spindles, for example, should all be left at their maximum possible length—22 inches—until you have bent the arm and bow, and test-fitted the spindles against them. In the same way, size the stretchers only after test-fitting the blanks between the legs.

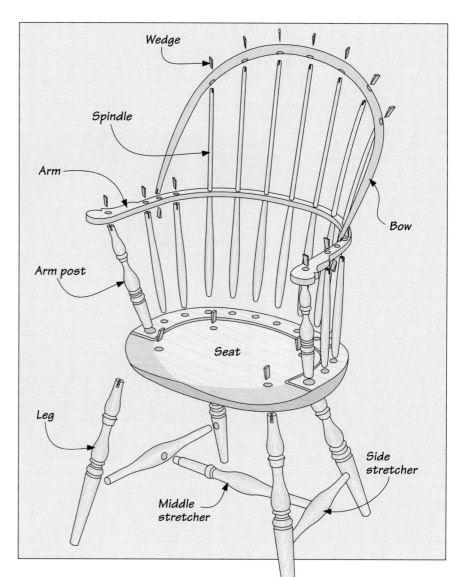

CUTTING LIST

PIECE	QTY.	THICKNESS	W. OR DIAM	L.
Arm	1	⁵⁄₈"	2"	44"
Arm posts	2		1¼"	11"
Bow	1		¾"	45"
Legs	4		1¾"	17"
Seat	1	2"	16"	20"
Long spindles	7		¾"	22"
Small spindles	4		¾"	11¾"
Middle stretcher	1		1¾"	17"
Side stretchers	2		1¾"	14½"

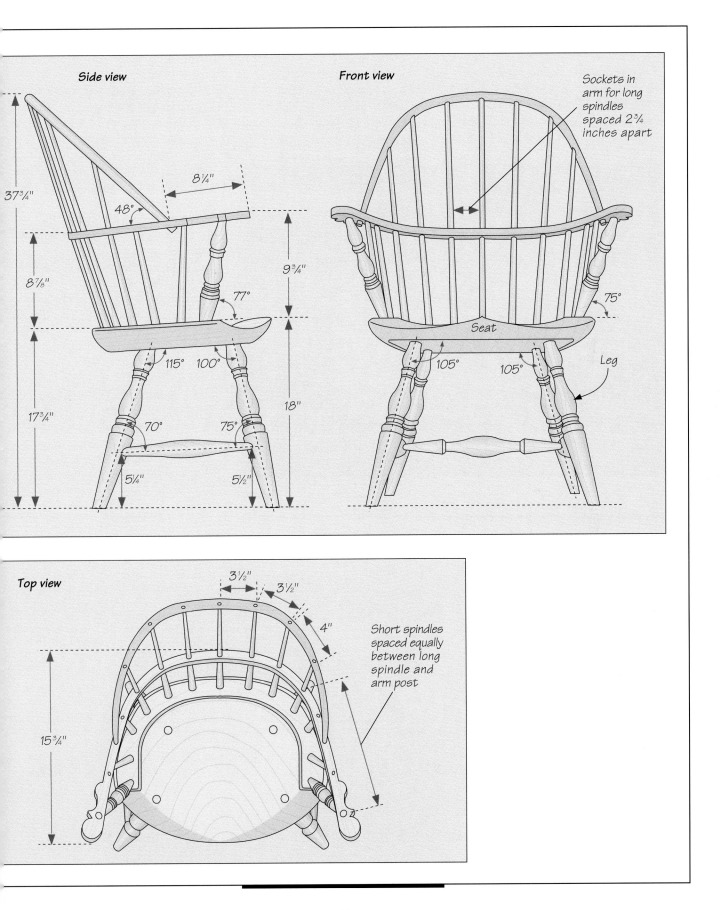

Side view

37¾"

48°

8¼"

8⅞"

77°

9¾"

115° 100°

18"

17¾"

70° 75°

5¼" 5½"

Front view

Sockets in arm for long spindles spaced 2¾ inches apart

75°

Seat

105° 105°

Leg

Top view

3½"

3½"

4"

Short spindles spaced equally between long spindle and arm post

15¾"

MAKING THE SPINDLES

Windsor chair making starts with a freshly cut log. Because green wood is swollen and lubricated with moisture, it is easy to cleave and bend. It is also less work to shape. Splitting wood from a log offers other advantages. First, it is stronger, because the break follows the wood fibers rather than shearing them, as a sawmill does. And second, wood seasons better if it is shaped while still green. A chair spindle, for example, will season more quickly and be less prone to cracking than a board, which may cup or check.

If you have access to a woodlot, you can fell your own trees using a chain saw. Otherwise, you may be able to obtain green logs from a sawmill, a local firewood supplier, or your local roads department. You can make an entire chair from hardwoods like hickory, white ash, or oak; but many woodworkers also use softwoods such as poplar and pine for the seat, which are easier to shape with hand tools.

The process described on the following pages for riving, or splitting, a log into spindle blanks can also be used to produce arm, leg, and stretcher blanks.

Once a log has been cut into manageable lengths, it is time to split it. Driving an iron wedge into the end of the log with a sledgehammer, as shown at left, will separate the wood fibers along the grain. Wear eye protection when you strike metal against metal.

PREPARING THE SPINDLE BLANKS

1 Splitting a bolt into quarters
Once you have felled a log and trimmed off the branches, saw it into workable lengths, called bolts. For best results, use a chain saw. Split the bolts in half *(photo, above)*, using a sledgehammer and iron wedges; wear safety goggles throughout the operation. To cleave the halves into quarters, stand the piece up, mark the center on the end and drive a wedge into the mark. Continue driving the wedge *(right)* until the bolt splits.

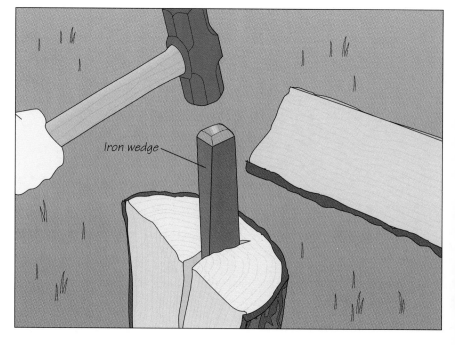

Iron wedge

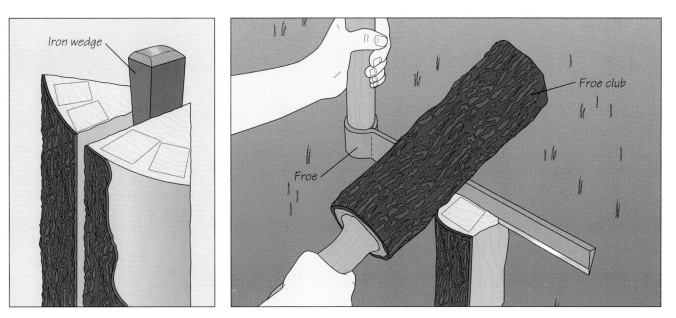

2 Riving a quarter bolt into blanks

Once you have split a bolt into quarters, rive each piece into spindle blanks. Outline the blanks on the end of the bolt and split it *(above, left)*, then rive the blanks with a froe and a froe club made from an 18-inch length of dense hardwood, such as maple, hickory, dogwood or elm. Holding the froe in one hand with the blade offset from the outline, strike the blade with the club *(above, right)*. Twist the froe back and forth, and drive it in deeper. Once the waste breaks off, repeat to make the remaining cuts.

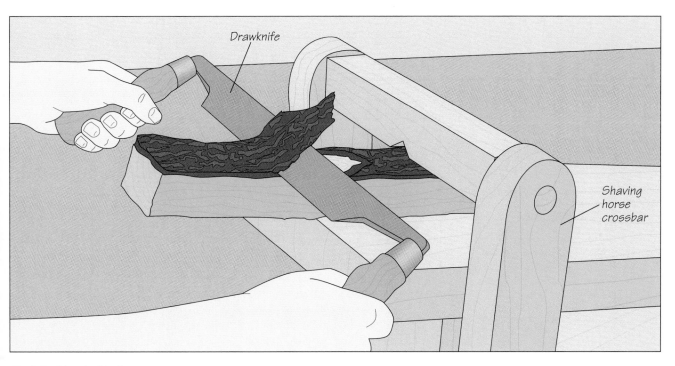

3 Debarking the blanks

Remove bark from your blanks using a drawknife on a shop-built shaving horse *(page 78)*. Secure the workpiece bark side up under the horse's crossbar. Then, holding the drawknife in both hands with the bevel down, pull the tool toward you to shave off the bark *(above)*. Turn the piece around to debark the other end.

ANATOMY OF SPINDLE

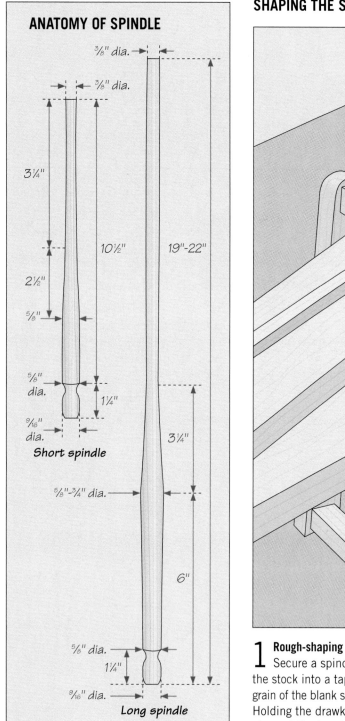

⅜" dia.

⅜" dia.

3¼"

10½"

19"–22"

2½"

⅝"

⅝" dia.

1¼"

⁹⁄₁₆" dia.

Short spindle

⅝"–¾" dia.

3¼"

6"

⅝" dia.

1¼"

⁹⁄₁₆" dia.

Long spindle

SHAPING THE SPINDLES

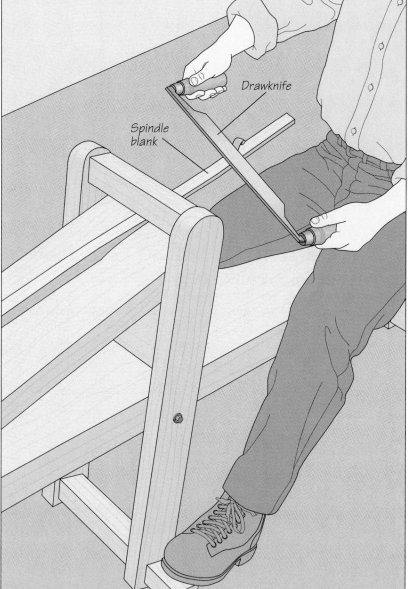

Drawknife

Spindle blank

1 Rough-shaping the spindles

Secure a spindle blank in your shaving horse and use a drawknife to shape the stock into a tapered cylinder. For best results, the growth rings on the end grain of the blank should be roughly vertical. Start by squaring and sizing the blank. Holding the drawknife on the blank bevel side down, pull the tool toward you, always following the grain *(above)*. Key dimensions and diameters for the seven long spindles and four short spindles you need for a chair are provided in the illustration at left. Turn the blank end-for-end and reposition it in the shaving horse frequently so you can shape it uniformly. Periodically check the piece's key diameters with calipers or a shop-made gauge like the one shown on page 77. (If you prefer, you can turn the spindles on a lathe, as shown on page 89.)

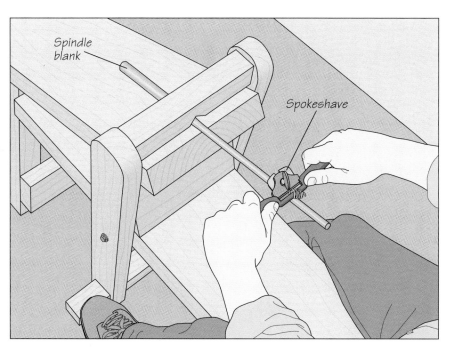

Spindle
blank

Spokeshave

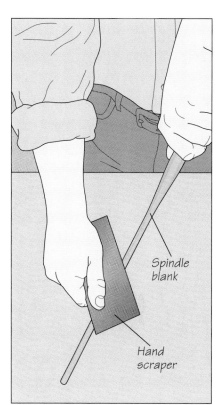

Spindle
blank

Hand
scraper

2 Evening out the spindles

Once all the spindles are rounded and tapered, use a spokeshave to even out their surfaces. Adjust the spokeshave for a very shallow cut. Handle the tool as you did the drawknife, always working with the grain *(above)* and repositioning the work-piece as necessary. Form the tenons at the bottom ends of the spindles with a knife, referring to the anatomy illustration opposite.

3 Smoothing the spindles

Use a hand scraper to give the spindles a smooth finish. Grasping the thick end of the spindle in one hand and, bracing the thin end on a work surface, use your other hand to draw the scraper along the surface *(above)*. Work in the direction of the grain and rotate the spindle frequently to keep it uniform.

SHOP TIP

Shop-made sizing gauge
A shop-made sizing gauge allows you to measure the diameters of chair spindles as you shape them. Bore holes into a wood scrap, sizing them according to the spindles' key diameters. Drill a ⁹⁄₁₆-inch-diameter hole into the gauge to check the tenon at the bottom end of the spindles, and a ³⁄₈-inch-diameter hole for the top end of the spindles. You can also check a key diameter along the length of the spindles by boring a hole through the gauge and slipping the blank into the hole. The blank is the correct diameter when it jams in the hole at the appropriate point along its length.

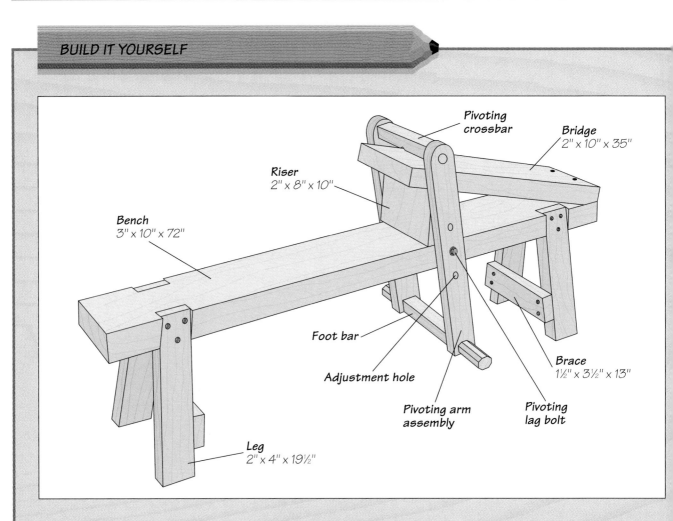

Pivoting
crossbar

Bridge
2" x 10" x 35"

Riser
2" x 8" x 10"

Bench
3" x 10" x 72"

Foot bar

Adjustment hole

Pivoting arm
assembly

Brace
1½" x 3½" x 13"

Pivoting
lag bolt

Leg
2" x 4" x 19½"

A SHAVING HORSE

The shaving horse grips stock securely in place while it is shaped with drawknives and spokeshaves. Simple to build, the typical shaving horse features a bench, an inclined bridge, and a pivoting arm assembly. By stepping down on the assembly's foot bar, you can lock your workpiece in position between the bridge and the assembly's crossbar.

To build the version shown above, start with the bench, which can be hewn from half a log 10 to 12 inches in diameter, or cut to length from rough 3-by-10 lumber. Make the length of the bench to suit your needs.

Next, cut the legs from 2-by-4 stock and attach them to the bench with angled T half-lap joints, reinforced by screws and braces *(right)*. Cut the two braces from 2-by-4 stock to fit between the leg's outside edges and screw them to the legs. To bevel the bottoms of the legs so they sit flat and level, set the shaving horse on a flat surface and butt a square board up against all four sides of each leg to mark cutting lines around them *(page 79, above, left)*. Saw the bottoms of the legs flat, then cut the tops of the legs flush with the bench.

Next, saw the riser and the bridge to size; the riser should be cut and beveled so that the bridge is inclined at an angle of about 15° to the bench. Locate the riser about 30 inches from the

back of the bench and screw it in place from underneath. Then screw the bridge to the riser *(page 79, above, right)* and the front of the bridge to the bench.

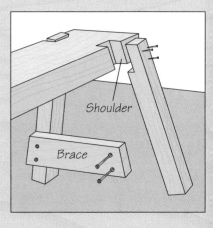

Shoulder

Brace

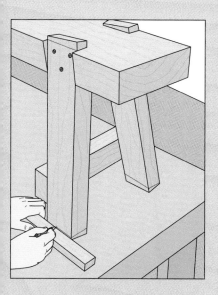

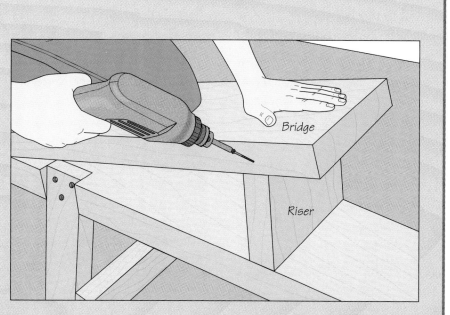

Next, build the pivoting arm. The assembly consists of two arms, a notched cross bar, and a foot bar (right). The crossbar is joined to the arms with through round mortise and tenons, while a bridle joint connects the foot bar to the arms. Cut the arms from 2-by-4 stock and bore two countersunk holes through each one for lag screws. Make additional holes through the arms above and below the first so you will be able to adjust the position of the assembly later to accommodate thicker stock. To prepare the arms for the bars, cut a round mortise through them at the top end and a notch at the bottom.

Next, cut the cross bar to length, making it about 3 inches longer than the width of the bench. Cut round tenons in both ends and a V-shaped notch in the middle of the bottom edge to hold your stock. Set the crossbar aside for now. Next, cut the foot bar, making its length twice that of the crossbar to provide an octagonal-shaped foot rest on each side of the arm assem-

bly. Cut dadoes in the foot bar to match the notches in the arms, fit the pieces together, and reinforce the joints with screws. With the foot bar attached, slip the arm assembly under the shaving horse and screw it in place with the

lag screws. Do not tighten the screws immediately; leave them loose enough so you can slip the crossbar in place. Do not glue or screw it, but leave the bar free to pivot. Once it is connected to the arms, finish tightening the lag screws.

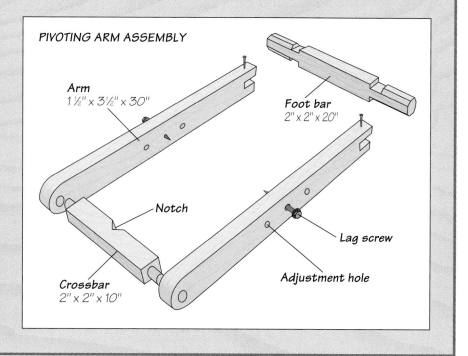

PIVOTING ARM ASSEMBLY

Arm
1 ½" x 3 ½" x 30"

Foot bar
2" x 2" x 20"

Notch

Lag screw

Crossbar
2" x 2" x 10"

Adjustment hole

MAKING THE BOW AND ARM

The arm and bow of the sack-back Windsor anchor the chair's backrest, tying the spindles into a strong and comfortable structure. The graceful curves of both pieces are achieved through steam bending, a process that may well be the most challenging part of making the chair.

The two essential elements of wood-steaming are a steam generator and an enclosed steamer. The version shown in the photo at right and described on page 83 is shop-made from ABS pipe. Be sure to make the steamer longer than the bow and arm, and seal it tightly to keep the steam from escaping. Include a small drain hole at one end and place the steamer on a slight incline, however, to allow the condensed steam to run out. If you are using a gas-powered steam source, it is safest to do your steaming outside. If you are using green wood, 15 to 20 minutes of steaming should make the piece sufficiently pliable to bend around a form. Air-dried lumber requires twice as much steaming. It will take about one week for a bent piece of 1-inch-thick stock to dry.

The arm of a sack-back Windsor chair is extracted from a steaming jig with a pair of tongs. The steaming process leaves the wood pliable for about a minute—long enough to bend the piece around a form. Because of the intense heat produced, always wear work gloves when handling steamed wood.

ANATOMY OF A BOW AND ARM

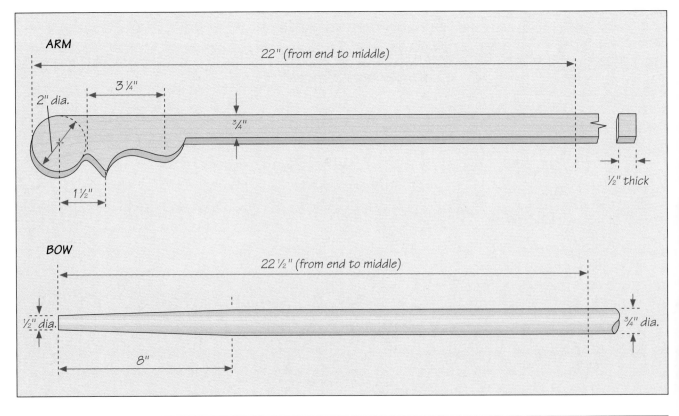

ARM

22" (from end to middle)

3 ¼"

2" dia.

¾"

1 ½"

½" thick

BOW

22 ½" (from end to middle)

½" dia.

¾" dia.

8"

PREPARING THE STOCK

1 Squaring the bow and arm

Drawknife the bow and arm roughly to size *(page 74)*, then use a bench plane to square the pieces and flatten their sides. Secure the blank between bench dogs on your workbench. Starting at one end of the stock, guide the plane across the surface to the other end; keep the sole of the tool flat on the workpiece and apply moderate downward pressure *(right)*. Plane the arm until it is ½ by ¾ inches; for the bow, refer to the anatomy illustration opposite.

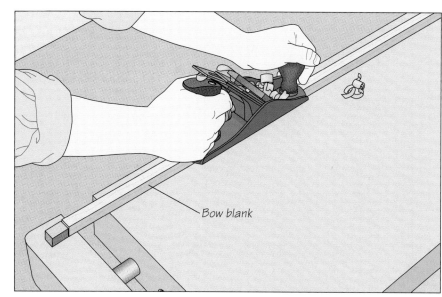

Bow blank

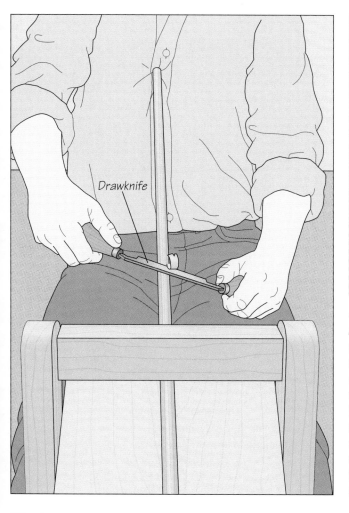

Drawknife

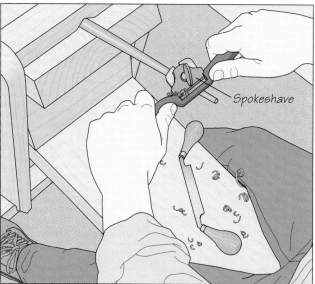

Spokeshave

2 Shaping the bow into a cylinder

Secure the bow blank in your shaving horse and start shaping the piece with a drawknife. Bracing the end of the stock against your chest, drawknife the blank into a cylinder *(left)*; work with the wood grain throughout. As shown in the diagram opposite, make the final diameter of the bow ¾ inch; it should taper down to ½ inch starting about 8 inches from each end. As you work on the thinner end of the workpiece, reposition the blank in the shaving horse so that less stock extends out from under the crossbar. Switch to a spokeshave to give the bow a smoother surface finish *(above)*, handling it as you did the drawknife.

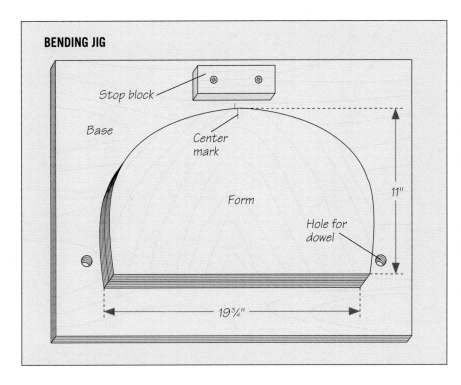

BENDING JIG

Stop block

Base

Center mark

Form

Hole for dowel

11"

19¾"

1 Building a bending jig

Build a bending jig like the one shown at left to bend the bow and arm of a sack-back Windsor chair. Cut two pieces of ¾-inch plywood to the desired curve of the bow and arm, then screw them together to make the form. Mount the form on a ¾-inch plywood base and mark the center of the form near its top edge. Then cut the stop block from hardwood and screw it to the base, and bore the two ¾-inch-diameter dowel holes into the base. The space between the block and dowels and the form should equal the thickness of the workpiece plus the wedges used to secure it in place. Finally, prepare the dowels and wedges, then clamp the base to a work surface.

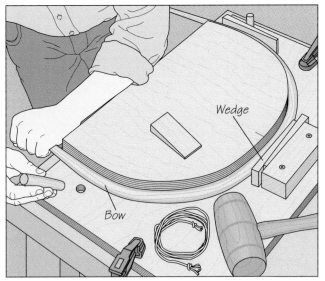

Wedge

Bow

2 Securing the bow around the form

Once the workpiece has been sufficiently steamed, remove it from the steamer (page 80) and place it on the bending jig. Align the middle of the bow with the center mark on the form and clamp the stock to the middle of the form by tapping wedges in place. Pull one end of the workpiece toward the form firmly and steadily until it contacts the side of the form. Insert a dowel into the hole in the base and tap in a wedge to secure the bow in place. Repeat for the other side of the workpiece (above). Work quickly to complete the bend.

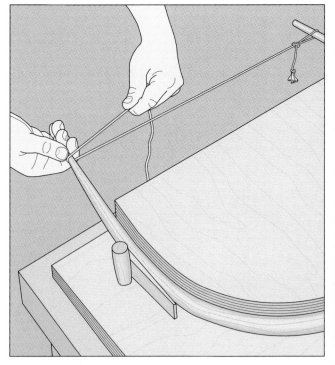

3 Maintaining the bend with string

Tie a length of string tightly between the ends of the bow (above) and begin steaming the arm. Once the arm is ready for bending, you can remove the bow and bend the arm as in step 2. The string will keep the bow bent until it dries.

A SHOP-MADE PIPE STEAMER

An economical and durable wood steamer like the one shown below can be fashioned from 2-by-4s and 4-inch-diameter ABS pipe and fittings. The device features support racks inside the pipe and a removable cap at each end for easy access. The steam source is a water can connected to the steamer by a length of plastic hose; the water in the can is heated by a propane-fired cooker. (This setup should only be used outdoors). The steam source should have a removable, screw-type cap.

To build the steamer, start with a length of schedule 80 ABS pipe longer than the bow and arm. Cut it in half and drill a series of holes through both pipe halves to accommodate ⅜-inch zinc-coated machine bolts and nuts

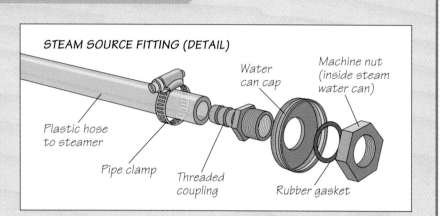

STEAM SOURCE FITTING (DETAIL)

Water can cap

Machine nut (inside steam water can)

Plastic hose to steamer

Pipe clamp

Threaded coupling

Rubber gasket

as shown. These bolts will support wood inside the steamer to prevent it from lying in condensed water. (The zinc coating will prevent the bolts from staining the wood). Drill the holes below the centerline of the pipe to provide room for the wood. Install the bolts, using steel and rubber washers

on both sides to make an airtight seal. Now glue both halves of the pipe to an ABS T connector. Drill a ½-inch drain hole at one end to release moisture and excess pressure. Then glue a connector pipe cut from 1½-inch ABS pipe to the spout of the T connector. Next, cut a length of plastic hose that will connect the steamer to the water can; the fittings required for the water can end are shown above. (The fittings for the steamer end of the hose are identical, except that an ABS end cap is used instead of the water can cap; the end cap is glued and screwed to the connector pipe.) Make sure the fittings are airtight. Lastly, build a 2-by-4 frame to support the steamer. Nail a small support block at one end so the steamer will rest on a slight incline and the excess water will run out of the drain hole.

To use the steamer, carefully connect the gas cooker to a propane tank. Fill the water can, attach the cap and hose to it, and set the can on the cooker. Secure the removable end caps on the steamer, light the cooker, and let the steamer build up steam. **(Caution: Do not let the steamer or steam source become pressurized.)**

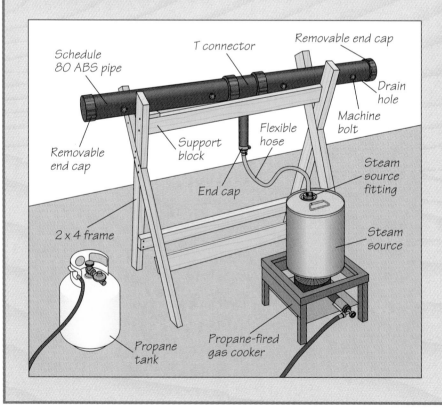

Schedule 80 ABS pipe

T connector

Removable end cap

Drain hole

Machine bolt

Removable end cap

Support block

Flexible hose

End cap

Steam source fitting

2 x 4 frame

Steam source

Propane tank

Propane-fired gas cooker

MAKING THE SEAT

A frame saw cuts a Windsor chair seat blank from a pine plank. The blank will be shaped later with a variety of hand tools. It could also be cut on a band saw.

The seat of a sack-back Windsor chair is best cut from a single plank. As shown in the photo at left, the blank is roughed out by hand with a frame saw or bowsaw. Then the seat is given its basic shape using a variety of hand tools—the edges are rounded over by a drawknife *(page 85)*, the top surface is scooped out with an adze and an inshave *(page 86)*, and some final touches are etched with a veiner *(page 87)*.

The final step is to bore mortises into the seat for the legs, spindles, and arm posts *(page 90)*. As shown in the anatomy illustration below, the arm post mortises are the largest: ⅞ inch in diameter; the leg mortises are ¾ inch in diameter, while the spindle mortises must be drilled with a ⅝-inch-diameter bit. Refer to the diagram for the seat's dimensions and for the location and spacing of the mortises.

SEAT DIMENSIONS AND ANGLES

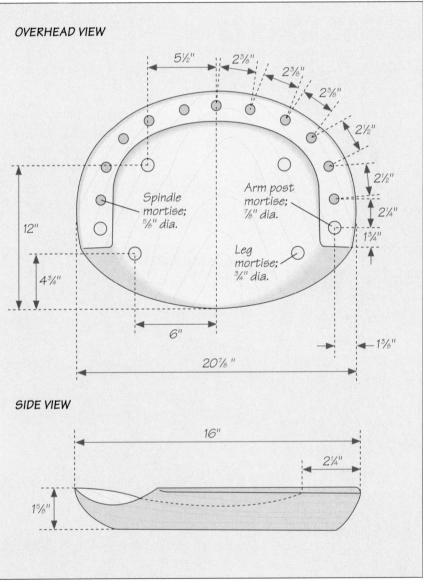

SHAPING THE SEAT

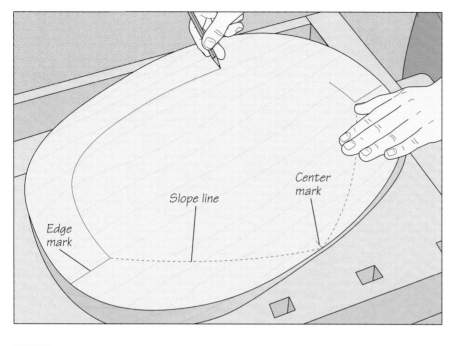

1 Outlining the top surface of the seat
Saw your seat blank from a piece of 2-inch-thick pine *(page 84)*, then outline the area to be scooped out. Start by marking the center of the blank's front edge. Next, mark a line 2¼ inches in from each side of the blank; the lines should be parallel to the front edge and 4¾ inches away from it. Draw a curved line that joins the two side marks and parallels the sides and back edge of the blank *(left)*. Finally, draw two curved lines that connect the side marks and the center mark at the front edge of the blank; these lines indicate where the top surface of the seat slopes toward the front edge and are represented by the dotted lines in the illustration.

Slope line

Center mark

Edge mark

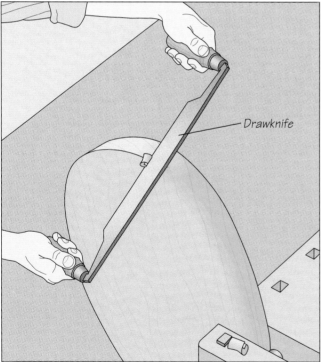

Drawknife

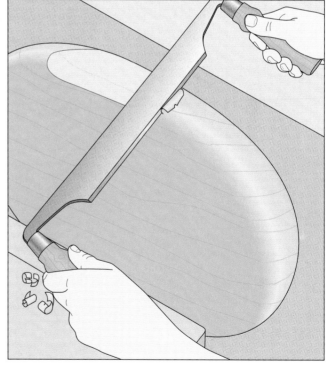

2 Rounding over the blank
Clamp the blank in a vise and use a drawknife to round over its edges. To begin, smooth the circumference of the blank and round over its underside, pulling the drawknife with the grain *(above, left)*; reposition the blank in the vise as necessary. If you encounter a knot in the wood, cut around it gradually, rather than trying to hack through it with a single stroke. Then use the drawknife to form the flat lip on the top surface along the front edge of the blank, angling the cut at about 40° *(above, right)*.

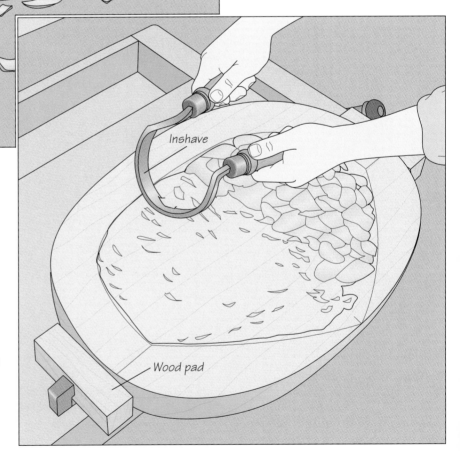

3 Dishing out the seat
Once the circumference of the seat has been shaped, rough out the waste from the top surface using a gutter adze. Wearing steel-toed boots, step on the edges of the blank to hold it steady and chop out the sitting area from one side of the outline to the other *(left)*. Try to cut with the grain, using short strokes. Make sure your feet are not in the path of the blade. Continue until you have cut about ¾ inch deep in the center of the seat with a gradual slope from the center up to the sides and front and back edges.

Gutter adze

Inshave

Wood pad

4 Smoothing the seat
Secure the seat between two bench dogs on your workbench, protecting the sides with wood pads. Start with an inshave to smooth the rough surface left by the adze. Working from one side of the top surface to the other, hold the inshave with both hands and pull it toward you; always follow the grain *(right)*. Use a convex spokeshave, or travisher, to refine the smoothness of the seat *(photo, page 71)*.

5 Shaping the lip

The lip at the front edge of the seat has a slight downward bevel. Working on one side of the seat's front edge at a time, use a small drawknife to cut the lip *(right)*. For maximum comfort, the transition between the dished out portion of the seat and the bevels should be smooth and gradual. The same should be true of the transition between the bevels and the flat section around the circumference of the seat. Finish smoothing the lip with a spokeshave.

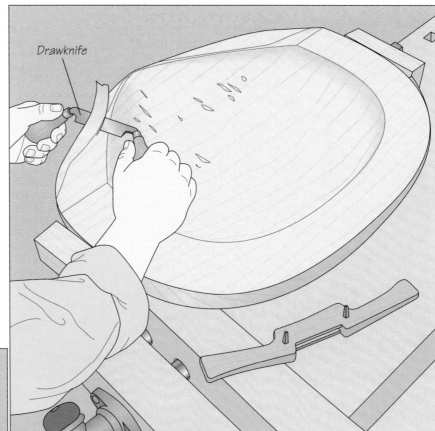

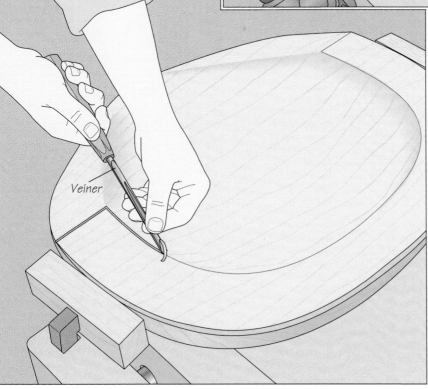

6 Carving the channel

Use a ¼-inch veiner to carve the channel that separates the seat's scooped-out top surface from the flat section around its circumference *(left)*. This is a decorative groove designed to sharpen the transition between the curved and flat portions of the seat.

MAKING THE LEGS, ARM POSTS, AND STRETCHERS

The legs, stretchers, and arm posts of a Windsor chair can be shaped with a drawknife, but many woodworkers work with a lathe instead, using a story pole for each component *(page 52)* as a

A hand brace fitted with a spoon bit bores a mortise in one side stretcher of a sack-back Windsor chair. The mortise will house a tenon of the middle stretcher. The mortise must be angled; a spoon bit enables you to start drilling the hole straight for the first ½ inch before tilting the tool to the correct angle.

guide to produce the turnings. Refer to the illustration below for dimensions, and use calipers to check key diameters as the work progresses. Start by turning the legs and the arm posts. But before you can turn the stretchers, you have to bore the leg mortises in the seat and test-fit the legs in place. By measuring the exact distance between the legs with the chair test-assembled, the stretchers can be sized with precision.

The tenons that join the pieces together—at the top ends of the legs, the bottoms of the arm posts, and at both ends of the stretchers—are tapered to lock the tenons into their mortises.

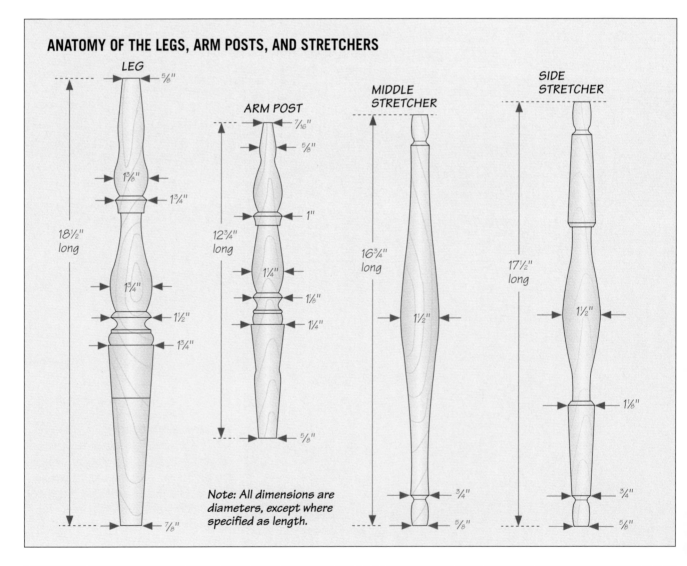

ANATOMY OF THE LEGS, ARM POSTS, AND STRETCHERS

LEG
⅝"
1⅜"
1¾"
18½" long
1¼"
1½"
1¾"
⅞"

ARM POST
7/16"
⅝"
1"
12¾" long
1¼"
1⅛"
1¼"
⅝"

MIDDLE STRETCHER
16¾" long
1½"
¾"
⅝"

SIDE STRETCHER
17½" long
1½"
1⅛"
¾"
⅝"

Note: All dimensions are diameters, except where specified as length.

TURNING THE LEGS AND ARM POSTS

1 Shaping the legs and arm posts

Mount the blank between centers on your lathe and use a roughing gouge to produce the turning. Refer to the anatomy illustration opposite for the locations and diameters of decorative elements like beads and coves. Once you are satisfied with the turning's shape, form the tapered tenon at the appropriate end *(right)*. On the legs, as shown, the tenon should be 2½ inches long, tapering from 1 inch to ⅝ inch in diameter. Make the arm post tenons 1 inch long, tapering from ⅝ to ⁷⁄₁₆ inch in diameter. Finally, turn a shallow groove on each leg to indicate the location of the stretchers; this groove will double as a decorative element.

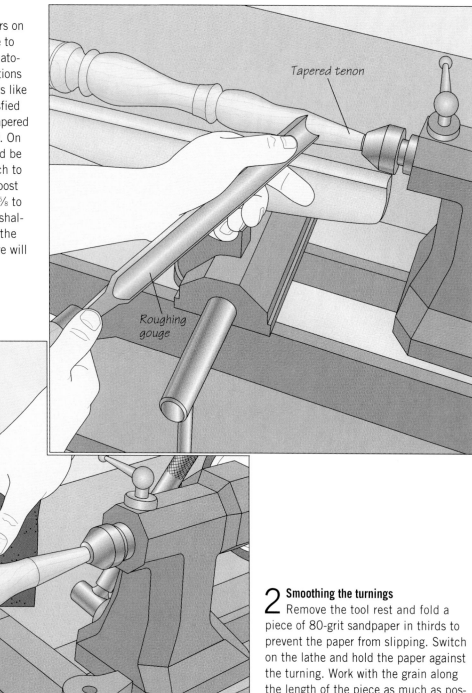

Tapered tenon

Roughing gouge

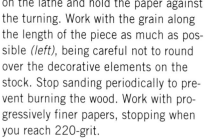

2 Smoothing the turnings

Remove the tool rest and fold a piece of 80-grit sandpaper in thirds to prevent the paper from slipping. Switch on the lathe and hold the paper against the turning. Work with the grain along the length of the piece as much as possible *(left)*, being careful not to round over the decorative elements on the stock. Stop sanding periodically to prevent burning the wood. Work with progressively finer papers, stopping when you reach 220-grit.

TURNING THE STETCHERS

1 Marking the leg and spindle mortises on the seat

Before you can turn the stretchers, you need to bore the leg mortises into the seat, test-fit the legs in the mortises, and measure the distances between the legs. Start by making a template of the seat from ¼-inch hardboard, referring to the anatomy illustration on page 84 for the dimensions of the seat as well as the location and size of the leg and spindle mortises. Drill a hole through the template at each mortise mark, then set the seat on a work surface, position the template atop it, and mark the holes *(right)*.

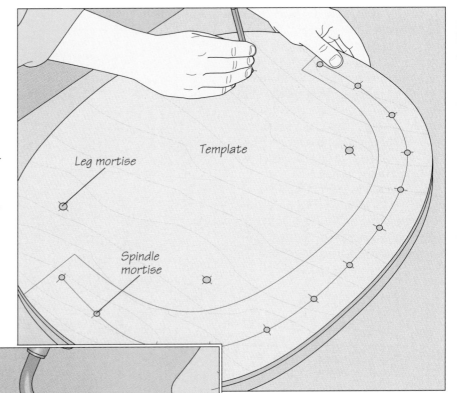

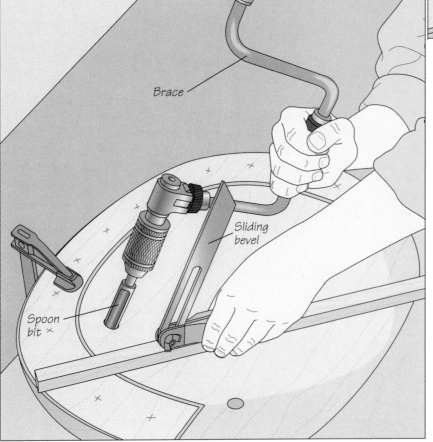

2 Drilling the leg mortises

Clamp the seat down and fit a hand brace with a spoon bit the same diameter as the small end of the leg tenons. Use a straightedge and a sliding bevel to help you drill the compound-angle holes. This will enable the legs to splay out from the side of the seat at the proper angle and be angled—or raked—toward the front or back of the chair. Position the straightedge across the seat at the correct splay angle of 105°, or 15° from the perpendicular *(page 73)*. Then adjust the sliding bevel to the required rake angle, which is 100° for the front legs and 115° for the rear legs, or 10° and 25° from vertical. Position the sliding bevel on the straightedge. Then, center the bit on the mortise mark and begin drilling, keeping the hand brace parallel to the straightedge and the bit lined up with the slope of the bevel *(left)*. Repeat the procedure to bore the remaining leg mortises.

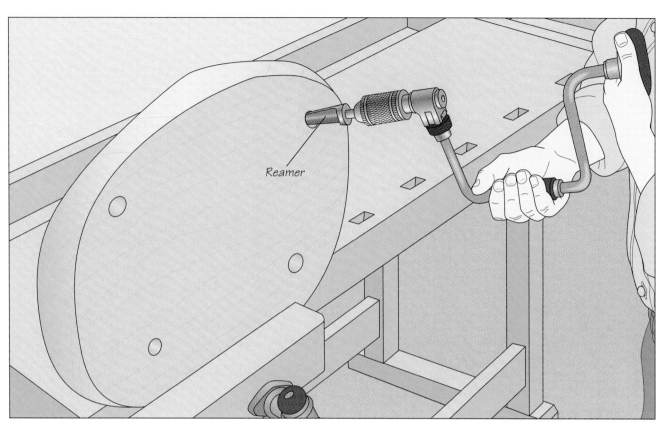

Reamer

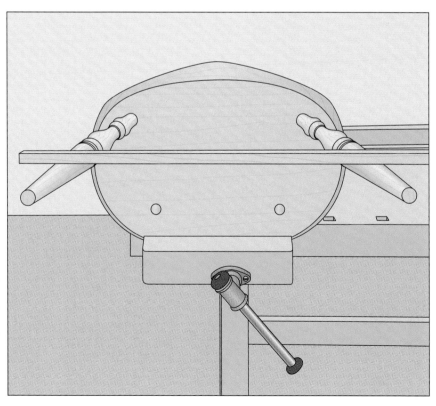

3 Tapering the leg mortises
Once all the leg mortises have been drilled, remove the spoon bit and install a tapered reamer. This device will give the leg mortises a tapered shape that matches the conical shape of the leg tenons, locking the legs to the seat. Secure the seat in a vise, then taper each leg mortise, steadying the hand brace against your chest *(above)*. Periodically test-fit the legs in their mortises, reaming the holes until the fit is snug.

4 Checking the splay and rake of the legs
Test-fit the front legs in their mortises and check whether their splay and rake angles are uniform. To help you gauge the rake angle, place a straightedge across the legs; the board should be perfectly level *(left)*. Repeat for the rear legs. If any of the angles are off slightly, you can compensate for minor inaccuracies when the time comes to turn and install the stretchers *(page 92)*.

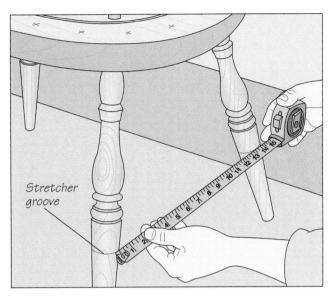

Stretcher
groove

5 Sizing the side stretchers

Set the seat-and-leg assembly on a work surface and measure the distance between the front and rear legs on one side *(above)*, aligning your tape measure with the stretcher grooves you turned in step 1. Repeat on the other side of the seat. To the longer of the two measurements, add 1¼ inches for the tenons at each end and an additional ¼ inch to hold the legs in tension when the chair is assembled. By sizing both stretchers according to the longer measurement, the rake angle of the two legs will equalize.

Side
stretcher

Spindle
gouge

6 Turning the side stretchers

Cut the side stretcher blanks to length and mount one between centers on your lathe. Shape the piece with a roughing gouge, referring to the anatomy illustration on page 88 for key diameters. Finish by turning the tenons at the ends with a spindle gouge *(above)*. Repeat for the other side stretcher.

7 Turning and sizing the middle stretcher

Since the middle and side stretchers are assembled before being glued to the legs, you cannot determine the length of the middle stretcher by measurement. Instead, calculate its length. Start by cutting a blank several inches longer than you need and turn it on your lathe; use the illustration on page 88 as a guide. To determine the stretcher's length, secure it in a vise and mark its middle. Then measure the distances between the front legs and then the rear legs, aligning your tape with the turned stretcher grooves; add the results together and divide by two. Add another 2½ inches for the tenons and ¼ inch to provide the proper amount of tension. Adjust a set of calipers to one-half your grand total and mark off this distance from the center mark to each end *(right)*. Cut the stretcher to length and turn a tenon at each end.

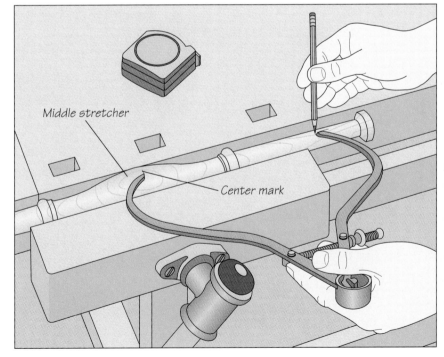

Middle stretcher

Center mark

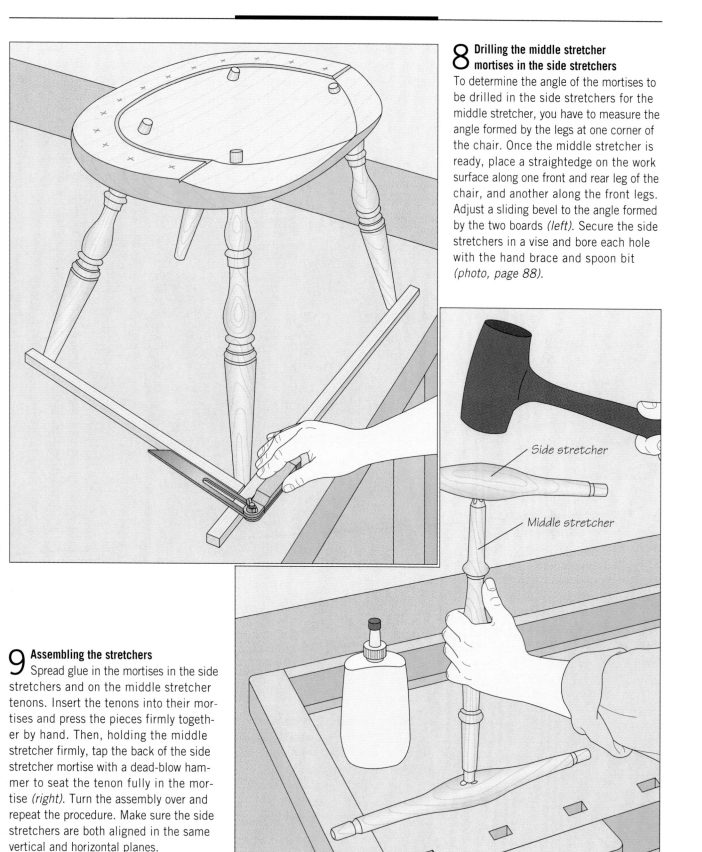

8 Drilling the middle stretcher mortises in the side stretchers

To determine the angle of the mortises to be drilled in the side stretchers for the middle stretcher, you have to measure the angle formed by the legs at one corner of the chair. Once the middle stretcher is ready, place a straightedge on the work surface along one front and rear leg of the chair, and another along the front legs. Adjust a sliding bevel to the angle formed by the two boards *(left)*. Secure the side stretchers in a vise and bore each hole with the hand brace and spoon bit *(photo, page 88)*.

Side stretcher

Middle stretcher

9 Assembling the stretchers

Spread glue in the mortises in the side stretchers and on the middle stretcher tenons. Insert the tenons into their mortises and press the pieces firmly together by hand. Then, holding the middle stretcher firmly, tap the back of the side stretcher mortise with a dead-blow hammer to seat the tenon fully in the mortise *(right)*. Turn the assembly over and repeat the procedure. Make sure the side stretchers are both aligned in the same vertical and horizontal planes.

ASSEMBLING THE CHAIR

Although the stretchers are glued to the legs and the legs are glued to the seat in separate steps, these procedures must be completed in quick succession for the chair to be symmetrical and well balanced. To make glue-up go easier, test-fit all the joints and correct any ill-fitting ones, then label the legs before applying any glue to the pieces.

Once the legs are fixed to the seat, the top ends of the legs are kerfed and wedges are inserted into the cuts to reinforce the joints *(page 96)*. The arm posts are installed next, then the arm is set in place, fastened to the arm posts with round mortise-and-tenons. The final steps of the assembly are installing the spindles and the bow *(page 98)*.

GLUING THE LEGS AND STRETCHERS TO THE SEAT

Once the stretchers have been glued to the legs and the legs fixed to the seat, it is time to trim the legs to the same length. The technique shown above involves cutting four wood blocks from a single board, then notching one of them to fit around a leg. Place the block around the first leg to be cut, then, holding the leg firmly with one hand, cut it to length with a flush-cutting saw. Once the first leg is trimmed, remove the notched block and replace it with one of the remaining blocks. Position the notched piece around the next leg and cut it. Continue in the same way until all four legs are cut.

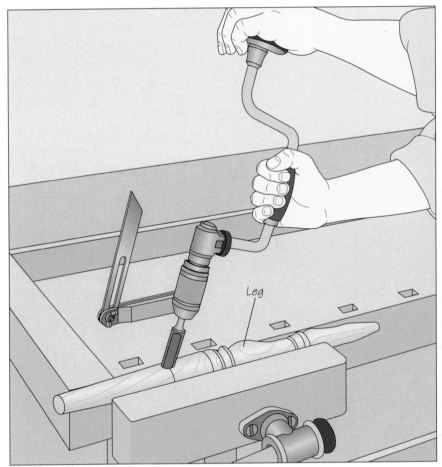

Leg

1 Drilling the stretcher mortises in the legs
With the chair test-assembled, position the side stretchers on the legs and mark their locations. Then remove the legs from the seat and secure one in a vise. Because the legs are raked to the front and back of the chair, the stretcher mortises in the legs must be angled. Adjust a sliding bevel to the correct angle, referring to the anatomy illustration on page 73. For the front legs the angle is 15° from the vertical; for the rear legs, it is 20°. Install a spoon bit in a hand brace, set the sliding bevel on the benchtop, and keep the brace aligned with the bevel blade as you drill each mortise *(above)*.

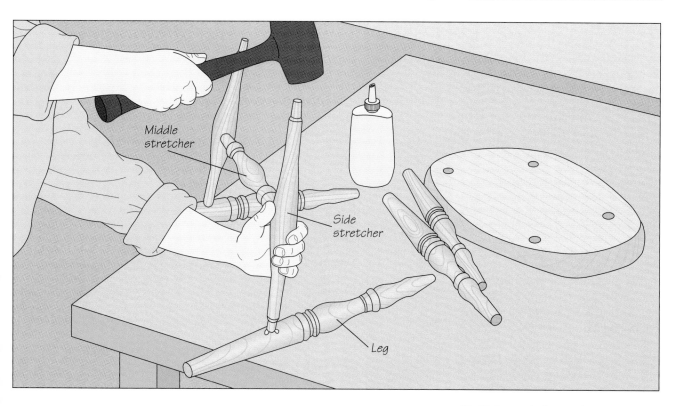

Middle
stretcher

Side
stretcher

Leg

2 Gluing up the legs and stretchers
Test-fit the legs and stretchers together, then spread glue on the stretcher tenons and in their corresponding mortises in the legs. Working on a flat surface, fit the pieces together; use a dead-blow hammer to seat the tenons fully in the mortises *(above)*.

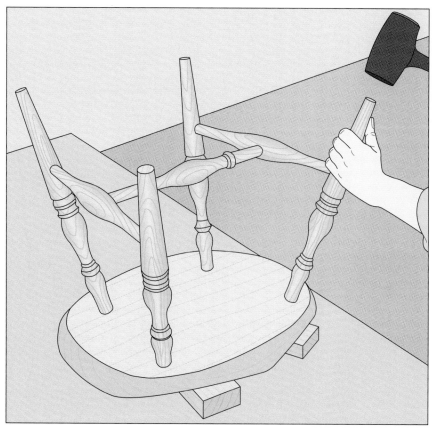

3 Gluing the legs to the seat
Since the leg tenons will protrude beyond the top surface of the seat when you drive them into their mortises, set the seat upside down on wood blocks on your work surface. Fit the legs into their mortises by hand, then finish the job with the dead-blow hammer *(left)*.

4 Kerfing the leg tenons for wedges

The leg tenons in the seat are wedged, tightening the joints and ensuring that the tenons will not loosen. Kerf the tenons by striking a firmer chisel with a hammer; to avoid splitting the seat, orient the slots so they are perpendicular to the grain of the seat *(right)*. Cut the kerfs to a depth slightly below the top of the seat.

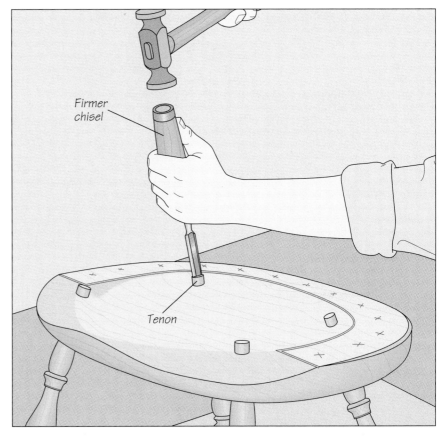

Firmer chisel

Tenon

5 Tapping in the tenon wedges

Cut hardwood wedges to fit into the kerfs; make them the same width as tenons, but a few inches longer, and no thicker than ¼ inch at the broad end. Coat the wedges with glue and drive them into the slots as far as they will go with a hammer *(below)*. Let the glue set, then trim the wedges even with the end of the tenons using a flush-cutting saw. Next, use a wide, shallow carving gouge to slice the tenons flush with the surface of the seat; strike the gouge with a wooden mallet *(inset)*. Finally, trim the legs to the same length *(photo, page 94)*.

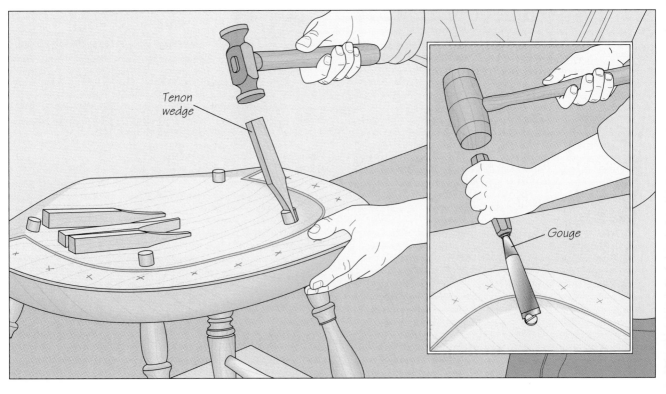

Tenon wedge

Gouge

INSTALLING THE ARM

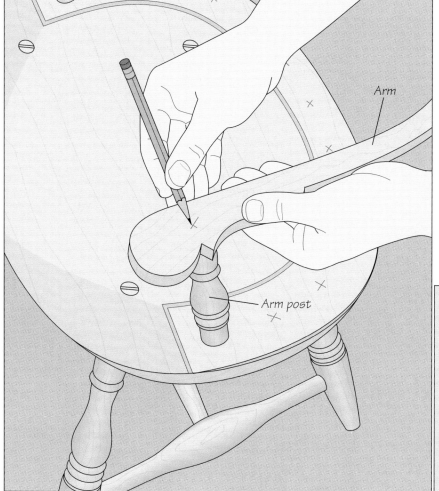

1 Marking the arm post mortises on the arm

Install the arm posts as you did the legs, referring to the anatomy illustration *(page 73)* for the angles at which the posts splay out to the sides and rake to the front of the seat. Drill the compound-angle mortises for the posts in the seat, then set the posts in place. Once the adhesive has set, position the arm on the posts and mark the location of the post tenons on the arm *(left)*. Make sure there will be at least ½ inch of solid stock all around the holes; reposition the arm and the posts, if necessary.

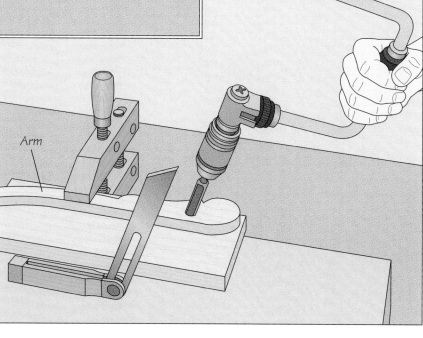

2 Boring the mortises for the arm posts

Clamp the arm to a work surface with a backup board under the stock to prevent tearout. To guide you as you drill the mortises in the arm, adjust a sliding bevel to the same rake angle used to bore the arm post mortise in the seat. Using a hand brace fitted with a spoon bit, start drilling the mortise with the tool at a 90° angle to the surface. Then tilt the brace back, keeping it aligned with the bevel blade to control the rake angle *(right)*; the splay angle can be eyeballed by referring to the arm post. Once both mortises are bored, taper them as you did the leg mortises in the seat *(page 91)*.

INSTALLING THE SPINDLES

1 Marking the center spindle location on the arm

Drill the spindle mortises in the seat; all these holes are at 90° to the seat surface. Then fit the arm onto the arm posts and insert the center spindle into its mortise in the seat. Adjust the position of the arm posts and arm, if necessary, until the assembly is symmetrical. Then holding the center spindle against the arm, mark its location on the top face *(right)*.

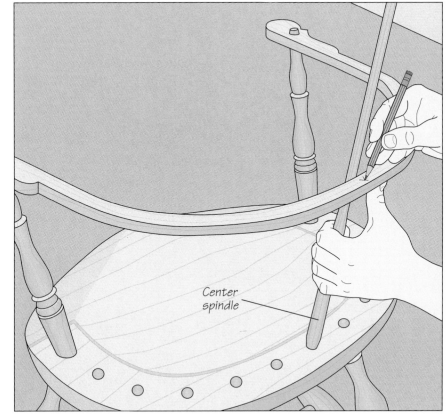

Center spindle

2 Marking the remaining spindle locations

Adjust a set of calipers to the distance between the center spindle and the adjacent ones *(page 73)* and mark their locations on the arm *(below)*. Repeat for the remaining long spindles. Mark the short spindles so the gap between them and the arm posts is equal.

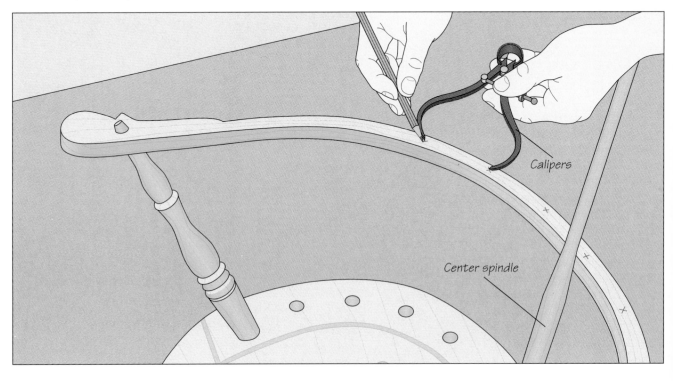

Calipers

Center spindle

3 Boring the spindle mortises in the arm

Clamp the arm to a work surface, centering a backup board under the hole you will be drilling. Also install a spoon bit in a hand brace and a small clamp on the edges of the stock in line with the hole mark to prevent the wood from splitting as you drill. Adjust a sliding bevel to the backward slant of the spindles, place it on the table, and align the bit with the bevel blade to bore the holes *(right)*.

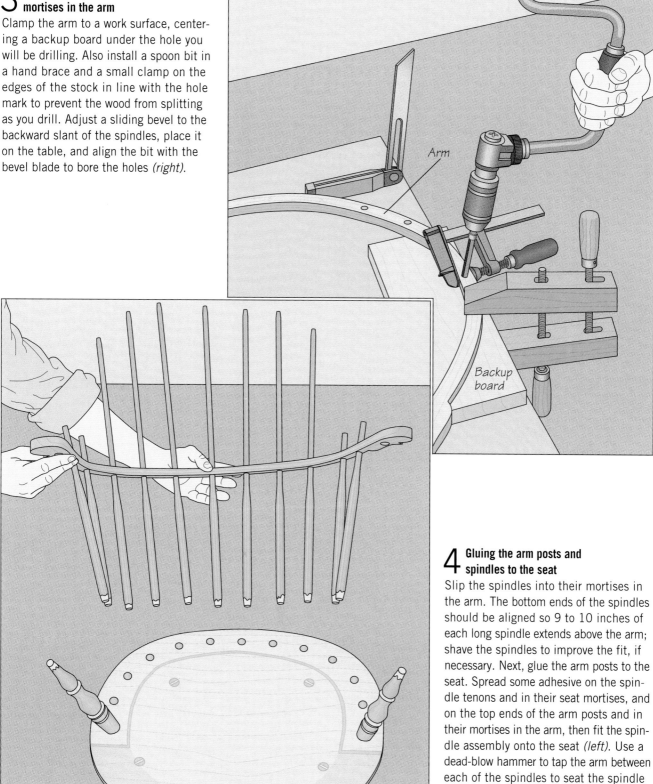

Arm

Backup board

4 Gluing the arm posts and spindles to the seat

Slip the spindles into their mortises in the arm. The bottom ends of the spindles should be aligned so 9 to 10 inches of each long spindle extends above the arm; shave the spindles to improve the fit, if necessary. Next, glue the arm posts to the seat. Spread some adhesive on the spindle tenons and in their seat mortises, and on the top ends of the arm posts and in their mortises in the arm, then fit the spindle assembly onto the seat *(left)*. Use a dead-blow hammer to tap the arm between each of the spindles to seat the spindle and arm post tenons fully in their mortises.

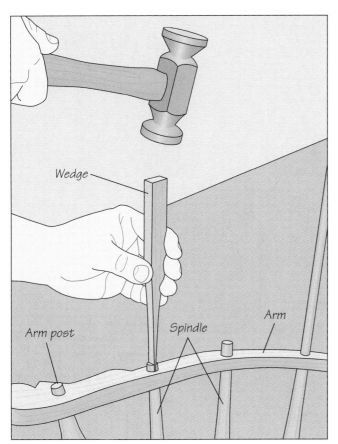

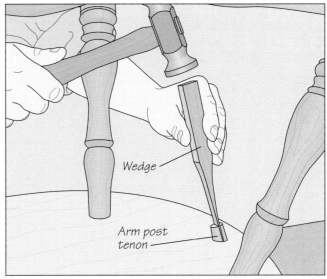

5 Wedging the arm posts and short spindles

The top ends of the short spindles and both ends of the arm posts are wedged in their mortises. Starting with the chair right-side up, chisel kerfs into the top ends of the short spindles and arm posts, making the cuts perpendicular to the wood grain of the arm, then tap a wedge into each cut *(left)*; follow the same procedure used for the leg tenons *(page 96)*. Turn the chair over and repeat to wedge the tenons at the bottom ends of the arm posts *(above)*. Trim the wedges and tenons flush with the seat surface.

INSTALLING THE BOW

1 Marking the bow ends on the arm

Position the bow on the arm and spindles so its ends extend below the arm by the same amount on both sides. To hold the bow steady while you mark its location on the arm, thread it in and out of the spindles *(right)*. Drill a hole at each marked point, centering the bit between the edges of the arm. Then taper the holes *(page 91)* to ensure a snug fit.

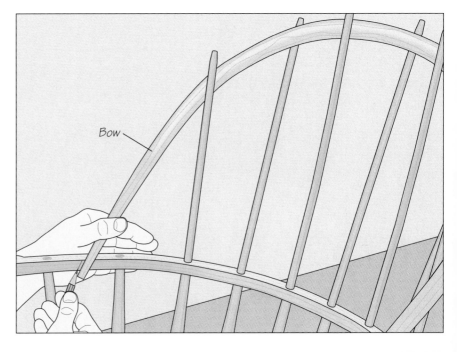

2 Boring the center spindle mortise through the bow

Mark the location of the center spindle on the bow, then drill a hole at your mark, using a hand brace and spoon bit *(right)*. Angle the hole to match the slant of the spindle.

3 Drilling the remaining spindle mortises

Referring to the anatomy illustration on page 73, use a pencil and a set of calipers to mark drilling points on the bow for the remaining spindles *(below)*. Then drill the holes.

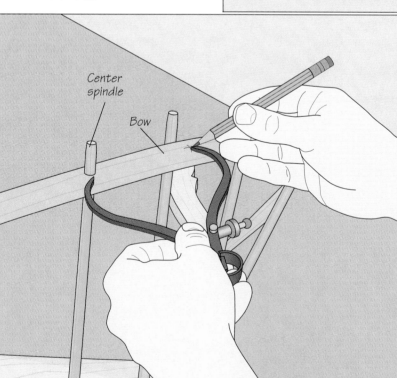

Center spindle

Bow

Center spindle

Bow

4 Gluing the bow to the arm and spindles
Spread glue in the spindle mortises in the bow and in the mortises for the bow in the arm. Fit the bow in position, tapping down along its length with a mallet to seat the piece fully *(right)*. Install wedges in the top ends of the spindles, repeating the procedure used for the short spindles *(page 100)*. Make sure the kerfs are perpendicular to the grain of the bow. Trim the wedges and spindles flush with the bow.

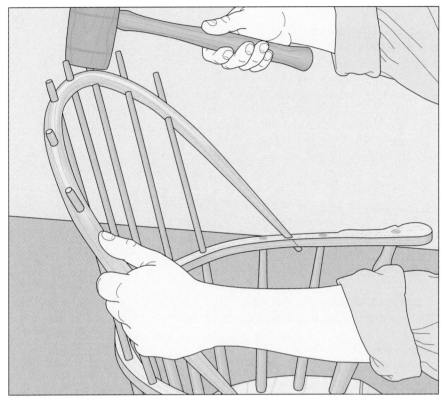

5 Wedging the ends of the bow
Once the glue securing the bow has cured, finish assembling the chair by wedging the ends of the bow. Set the chair upside down on a work surface, clamping down the arm so the ends of the bow extend off the table by a few inches. Then kerf the ends of the bow and glue in wedges, tapping in each one with a hammer *(below)*.

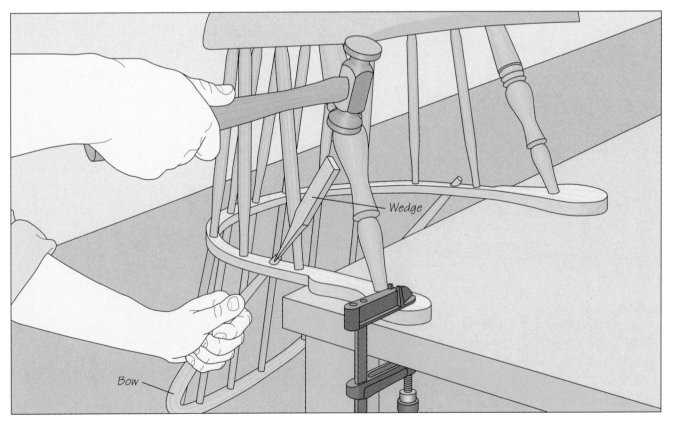

Wedge

Bow

A MILK PAINT FINISH

The traditional finish for Windsor chairs is milk paint, which is thin enough to allow wood grain to show through. You can buy the paint in powdered form and mix it with water or make your own by following the recipe presented below. The blend provided was used in colonial times as an interior wall paint, which yielded a flat, lusterless finish that can be stained, oiled, or waxed once the surface is dry. To produce a semigloss sheen, egg whites can be added to the recipe. Their use has a long tradition in painting; egg tempera paints were used by some of the great Renaissance masters.

The ability of milk paint to produce a finish that is both durable and moisture-resistant is somewhat of a mystery, but it is known that a chemical reaction occurs between the lactic acid in the milk and the lime, which is a base; lime is not simply added as a thickener. Skim milk is used because the fat in whole milk interferes with the curing process, reducing the paint's durability. Buttermilk or the whey from cheese-making were traditional substitutes for whole milk.

A milk paint finish is being brushed onto a sack-back Windsor chair. The transparency of milk paint, compared to other paints, along with its tendency to vary slightly in hue across a surface, complements the hand-sculpted contours of the Windsor chair. The dark green shown at right is a traditional color for Windsors.

PREPARING A MILK PAINT FINISH

Combining and applying the ingredients

To make about 2 quarts of milk paint, wear gloves and pour 3 cups of skim milk into a container *(above)*. Sprinkle 2 ounces of slaked lime into the milk and mix for 3 minutes. Then stir in 16 ounces of plaster of Paris. Add coloring, such as artist's pigments or earth pigments used for coloring cement, or powdered chalk like the kind used in chalk lines. To thicken the solution, add more plaster of Paris. Test the paint on a scrap piece and let it dry. To deepen the hue of the finish, add more coloring. Let the paint sit for 1 hour, then brush it on, stirring frequently. Since milk paint raises the grain of the wood, sand the surface lightly between coats for a smooth finish. Add a thin layer of varnish, shellac, oil, or wax to protect the finish.

QUEEN ANNE SECRETARY

The weight of the fall-front in the secretary shown above is borne by a pair of supports called lopers. In the down position, the front becomes a leather-lined writing surface. The removable pigeonhole unit is set atop the desk unit.

T he secretary, a bookcase and slant-top desk combination, evolved in Britain and America in the 18th Century and has been popular ever since. By setting a bookcase atop a slant-top desk, the secretary embodies the close relationship between books and writing. Until the 19th Century, books were an expensive and sometimes rare commodity to be treasured. A secretary offered an ideal way to keep a precious collection safely behind glass, only an arm's reach away. The Queen Anne version featured in this chapter is more elegant than the stolid furniture that hallmarked the 17th Century, but it is less ornate than some of the incarnations that followed it, such as Chippendale-style secretaries.

The desk half of the piece has several useful features. The veneered fall-front can be lowered to become a large writing surface and reveal the "pigeonhole" unit. This network of dividers, compartments, and drawers served as a primitive precursor to today's laptop computers. Completely portable, the unit enabled clerks in bygone days to take their offices and information with them when traveling. You can adapt the pigeonhole design shown on page 108, adding or removing compartments, adjusting their spacing, or incorporating more drawers to fit your needs.

Another useful component of the desk is the lockable lid. This safeguards the contents of the pigeonholes, while providing a quick way to hide clutter behind the fall-front.

Both the desk and bookcase derive much of their strength from half-blind dovetails. Cutting these joints by hand *(page 109)* is time-consuming, but well worth the effort, considering the hand-crafted appearance you will obtain. The drawers can be made with through dovetails cut with a commercial jig and a router *(page 116)*, and the end grain of the tails hidden with false fronts. You can also use half-blind dovetails to attach the drawer fronts, thereby dispensing with false fronts.

The veneer applied to the fall-front *(page 121)* adds a decorative flair to the desk, becoming the focus of the entire piece. The secretary shown opposite uses bookmatched veneer, but other attractive options are shown on page 124. If you plan to do a lot of veneering, consider buying a vacuum press *(page 124)*; otherwise, use a shop-made veneer press *(page 125)*.

The design and construction of the base *(page 128)* and crown molding *(page 134)* may appear complicated, but the time-tested methods presented are not difficult to master and are important to accommodate the inevitable wood movement at these vulnerable locations.

Made from mahogany with a clear lacquer finish, the Queen Anne secretary shown at left marries elegance with usefulness, crowning a slant-top desk with a bookcase to create a single, striking piece of furniture.

ANATOMY OF A QUEEN ANNE SECRETARY

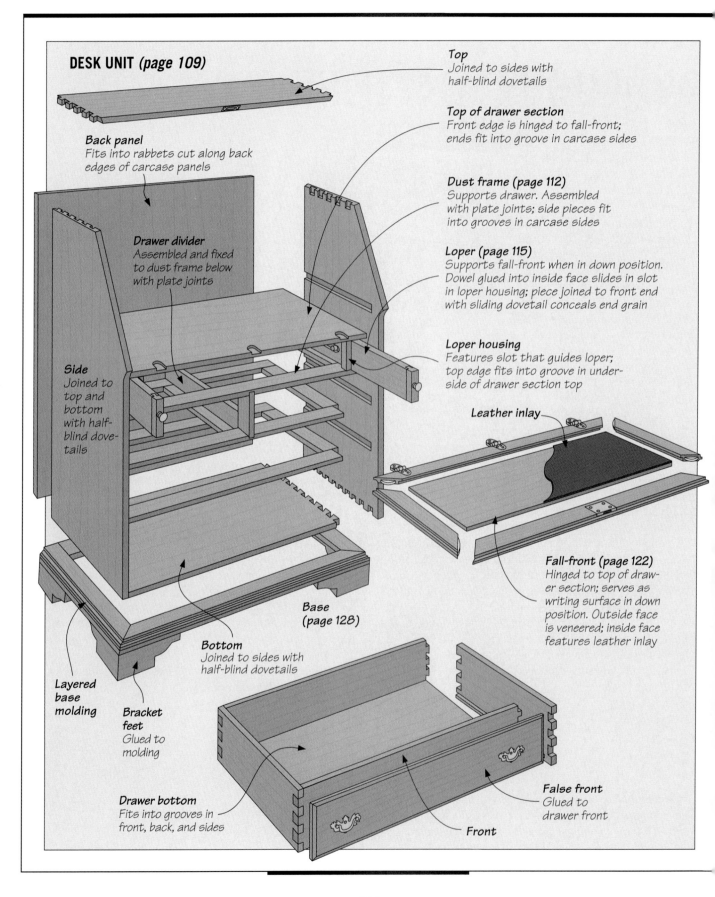

DESK UNIT *(page 109)*

Top
Joined to sides with half-blind dovetails

Top of drawer section
Front edge is hinged to fall-front; ends fit into groove in carcase sides

Back panel
Fits into rabbets cut along back edges of carcase panels

Dust frame (page 112)
Supports drawer. Assembled with plate joints; side pieces fit into grooves in carcase sides

Drawer divider
Assembled and fixed to dust frame below with plate joints

Loper (page 115)
Supports fall-front when in down position. Dowel glued into inside face slides in slot in loper housing; piece joined to front end with sliding dovetail conceals end grain

Side
Joined to top and bottom with half-blind dovetails

Loper housing
Features slot that guides loper; top edge fits into groove in underside of drawer section top

Leather inlay

Base (page 128)

Bottom
Joined to sides with half-blind dovetails

Fall-front (page 122)
Hinged to top of drawer section; serves as writing surface in down position. Outside face is veneered; inside face features leather inlay

Layered base molding

Bracket feet
Glued to molding

Drawer bottom
Fits into grooves in front, back, and sides

False front
Glued to drawer front

Front

The major components of the Queen Anne secretary are shown in exploded form in this section. The most elaborate part—the desk unit *(page 106)*—is essentially a carcase with drawers, a fall-front and an opening for the pigeonhole unit. All the corner joints for the carcase, the bookcase, and the drawers are dovetailed. The drawers are supported by dust frames attached to the sides. To allow for wood movement as a result of changes in humidity, the frames are glued to the sides only near the front; screws driven through elongated holes reinforce this connection. The fall-front is fixed to the unit with butt hinges. To ease the strain on the hinges when the fall-front is let down, a pair of boards, called lopers, slide out to provide support.

The bookcase *(below)* is another solid-panel carcase with shelves, a back panel, and crown molding. The shelves are fully adjustable; they sit on pins that can be inserted at any height in the sides. The glass doors that grace the bookcase and protect its contents are hinged to the side panels.

The pigeonhole unit *(page 108)* is a smaller carcase with three drawers and a series of vertical dividers. The unit rests atop the drawer section of the desk, with strips of molding concealing the gap between the two.

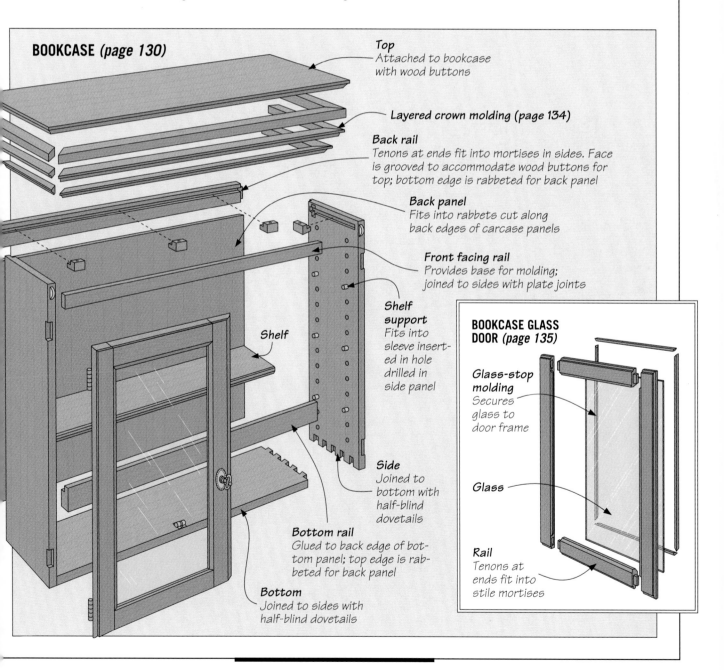

BOOKCASE *(page 130)*

Top
Attached to bookcase with wood buttons

Layered crown molding (page 134)

Back rail
Tenons at ends fit into mortises in sides. Face is grooved to accommodate wood buttons for top; bottom edge is rabbeted for back panel

Back panel
Fits into rabbets cut along back edges of carcase panels

Front facing rail
Provides base for molding; joined to sides with plate joints

Shelf

Shelf support
Fits into sleeve inserted in hole drilled in side panel

Side
Joined to bottom with half-blind dovetails

Bottom rail
Glued to back edge of bottom panel; top edge is rabbeted for back panel

Bottom
Joined to sides with half-blind dovetails

BOOKCASE GLASS DOOR *(page 135)*

Glass-stop molding
Secures glass to door frame

Glass

Rail
Tenons at ends fit into stile mortises

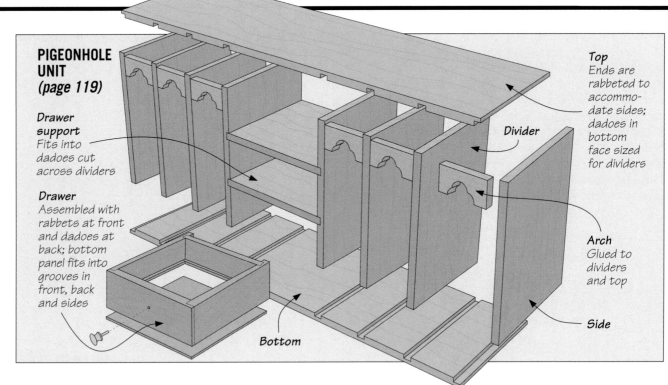

PIGEONHOLE UNIT
(page 119)

Drawer support
Fits into dadoes cut across dividers

Drawer
Assembled with rabbets at front and dadoes at back; bottom panel fits into grooves in front, back and sides

Top
Ends are rabbeted to accommodate sides; dadoes in bottom face sized for dividers

Divider

Arch
Glued to dividers and top

Side

Bottom

CUTTING LIST

	T	W	L
BUREAU: Fall Front			
1 Panel	⅜	10¼	29½
2 Rails	¾	2¼	14
2 Stiles	¾	2¼	33⅛
BUREAU: Carcase			
2 Sides	¾	17½	38
1 Top	¾	10⅞	33⅛
1 Bottom	¾	17½	33⅛
1 Back Panel	¼	32¾	37¼
1 Writing surface	¾	17½	32½
2 Lopers	¾	3¾	17
2 Loper housings	¾	3¾	17
6 Dust frame stiles	¾	2	32½
6 Dust frame rails	¾	2	13¼
1 Cross rail	¾	4	13¼
1 Drawer divider	¾	2	15¼
1 Muntin	¾	2	5
BUREAU: Base			
1 Molding front	¾	⅞	35¾
2 Molding sides	¾	⅞	18⅜
1 Molding base front	¾	3	35¾
2 Molding base sides	¾	3	19⅛
1 Molding frame front	¾	2	34

	T	W	L
1 Molding frame back	¾	2	30
2 Molding frame sides	¾	2	17½
6 Bracket feet	¾	3	8
BUREAU: Deep Drawers			
4 Upper front and back	¾	4¹⁵⁄₁₆	15¾
4 Upper sides	¾	4¹⁵⁄₁₆	17
2 Upper false fronts	¾	5	15⅞
2 Upper drawer bottoms	¼	15	16½
2 Middle front and back	¾	5¹⁵⁄₁₆	32⅜
2 Middle sides	¾	5¹⁵⁄₁₆	17
1 Middle false front	¾	6	32½
2 Lower front and back	¾	6¹⁵⁄₁₆	32³⁄₈
2 Lower sides	¾	6¹⁵⁄₁₆	17
1 Lower false front	¾	7	33½
2 Drawer bottoms	¼	31½	16½
BUREAU: Shallow Drawer			
2 Front and back	¾	3¹¹⁄₁₆	29⅛
2 Sides	¾	3¹¹⁄₁₆	17
1 False front	¾	3¾	29¼
1 Drawer bottom	¼	28⅜	16½
BUREAU: Pigeonhole Unit			
2 Top and bottom	½	8½	32½
8 Dividers and sides	½	8½	10½

	T	W	L
2 Drawer supports	½	8½	9¼
6 Arches	½	1½	3¼
3 Drawer fronts	½	3	8½
3 Drawer backs	½	3	8
6 Drawer sides	½	3	8½
3 Bottoms	½	8	8
BOOKCASE: Carcase			
2 Sides	¾	8½	35¼
1 Top	¾	11¾	38
1 Bottom	¾	8½	32⅛
1 Front facing rail	¾	3¼	33
1 Back rail	¾	3	31½
1 Bottom Rail	¾	2	31½
1 Molding frame front	¾	2	36½
2 Molding frame sides	¾	2	11
1 Molding front (built up)	1¼	1¼	35¾
2 Molding sides	1¼	1¼	10¾
1 Back panel	¼	29½	32¾
BOOKCASE: Doors			
4 Stiles	¾	2	31¾
4 Rails	¾	2	12½
1 Glass-stop molding	¼	¼	192
2 Glass panes	⅛	12⁵⁄₁₆	27⅞

MAKING THE DESK UNIT

The carcases of the desk unit and bookcase form the two main parts of the secretary. In keeping with the twin requirements of elegance and usefulness, both pieces are assembled with one of the most attractive—and sturdy—joints available to the woodworker: the half-blind dovetail. The steps shown below and on the following pages feature the connection between the top and sides of the desk unit; but the same procedures apply to the joints at the bottom of the both the desk and bookcase units.

Once the dovetails have been cut, you can move on to making the dust frames *(page 112)* and the loper housings. The carcase is then assembled *(page 113)* and the back panel is nailed in place *(page 115)*. The final step, once the glue has cured, is installing the lopers.

A plate joiner cuts a slot in the stile of a dust frame; a stop block clamped in place holds the workpiece square to the tool. A wood biscuit and glue will be added to the semicircular cut and then fitted into a mating slot in a rail. Quick and easy to make, the resulting joint will be strong and invisible, enabling the frame to support a drawer.

CUTTING HALF-BLIND DOVETAILS

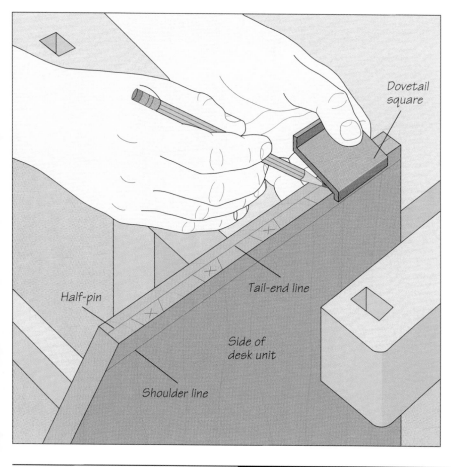

Dovetail square

Half-pin

Tail-end line

Side of desk unit

Shoulder line

1 Marking the pins in the sides
Once you have glued up the panels and cut them to the right size, mark their outside faces with an X. Secure one of the side panels upright in a vise, then set a cutting gauge to about two-thirds the thickness of the sides and mark a line across the end to indicate the end of the tails. The line should be closer to the outside than the inside face of the panel. Adjust the cutting gauge to the stock thickness and scribe a line on the inside face of the side to mark the shoulder line of the tails. Next, use a dovetail square to outline the pins on the ends of the side; the wide part of the pins should be on the inside face of the panel *(left)*. There are no strict guidelines for spacing dovetail pins, but for stock of the dimensions provided on page 108, 1¼-inch evenly spaced pins with ⅝-inch tails and a half-pin at each edge will make for a strong and attractive joint. To complete the marking, extend the lines on the panel end to the shoulder line on its inside face. Mark the waste sections with Xs as you go.

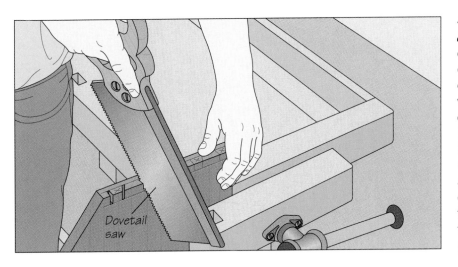

2 Cutting the pins

Leaving the side panel in the vise, cut along the edges of the pins with a dovetail saw *(left)*, working your way from one panel edge to the other. (Some wood-workers prefer to cut all the right-hand edges first, then all the left-hand edges.) Hold the panel steady and align the saw blade just to the waste side of the cutting line; angle the saw toward the waste to avoid cutting into the pins. Use smooth, even strokes, allowing the saw to cut on the push stroke. Continue the cut just to the shoulder line, then repeat to saw the pins at the other end of the panel.

Dovetail saw

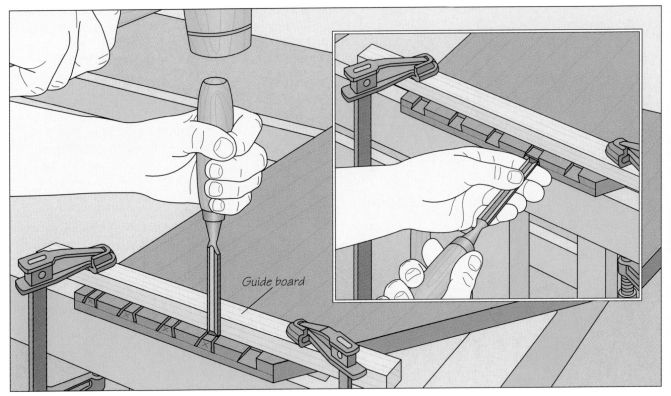

Guide board

3 Chiseling out the waste

Set the panel inside-face up on a work suface and clamp a guide board to it, aligning its edge with the waste side of the shoulder line. Starting at one edge of the stock, hold the flat side of a chisel against the guide block; the blade should be no wider than the narrowest part of the waste section. With the chisel perpendicular to the face of the board, strike the handle with a wooden mallet, making a 1/8-inch-deep cut into the waste *(above)*. Then hold the chisel bevel up and square to the end of the board about 1/8 inch below the top surface and peel away a thin layer of waste. Continue until you reach the scribed line on the end of the board, then repeat the process with the remaining waste sections. Pare away any excess waste from between the pins, completing work on one waste section before moving to the next. Press the flat side of the chisel against the bottom of the section with the thumb of your left hand; with your right hand, push the chisel toward the shoulder line, shaving away the last slivers of waste *(inset)*. Then pare away any waste from the sides of the pins.

4 Laying out the tails

Set the top panel outside-face down on the work surface and scribe a shoulder line the thickness of the stock from the end of the workpiece. Secure a side panel in a handscrew, then hold the panel top-end down with its inside face aligned with the line on the top panel. Making certain that the straight edges of the boards are flush, clamp the handscrew to the bench. Outline the tails with a pencil *(right)*, then extend the lines on the panel end using a try square. Mark all the waste section with Xs.

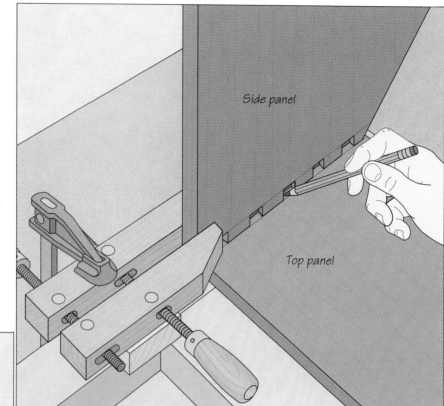

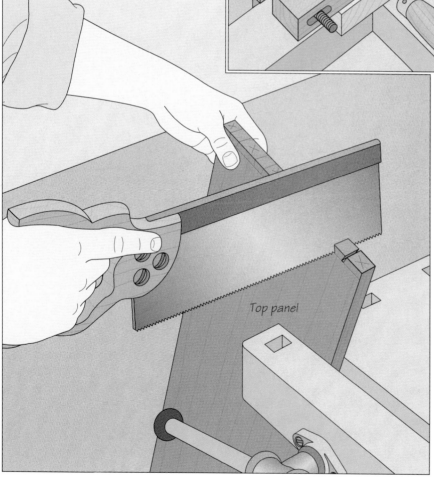

5 Cutting the tails

Use a dovetail saw to cut the tails the same way you sawed the pins *(step 2)*. Angling the board, as shown at left, rather than the saw, makes for easier, more accurate, cutting. Secure the panel so the right-hand edges of the tails are vertical. Saw smoothly and evenly along the edges of the tails, stopping at the shoulder line. Reposition the panel in the vise to cut the left-hand edges. Once all the saw cuts have been made, remove the waste with a chisel as in step 3. To avoid splitting the tails, remove about half the waste, then turn the panel over to chisel out the remaining waste.

MAKING THE DUST FRAMES

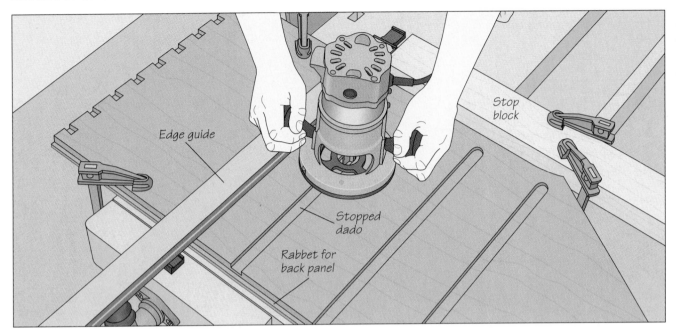

Edge guide

Stop block

Stopped dado

Rabbet for back panel

1 Dadoing the carcase sides

Use a router to cut ⅜-inch-wide, ³⁄₁₆-inch-deep rabbets around the back edge of the carcase to accommodate the back. Then prepare the sides for the dust frames. The ends of the frames fit into stopped dadoes in the sides. To cut the dadoes, install a ¾-inch straight bit in your router, set the cutting depth to ¼ inch, and secure one of the side panels inside-face up to a work surface. Refer to the anatomy illustration on page 106 and the drawer measurements on page 108 to outline the dadoes on the stock, then clamp an edge guide to the panel so the bit will be centered on the first marked line. Also clamp a stop block along the front edge of the panel so the dado will stop 2 inches short of the edge. For each dust frame, rout a stopped dado from the back edge of the side panel *(above)*, stopping when the router base plate contacts the stop block. Square the ends of the dado with a chisel.

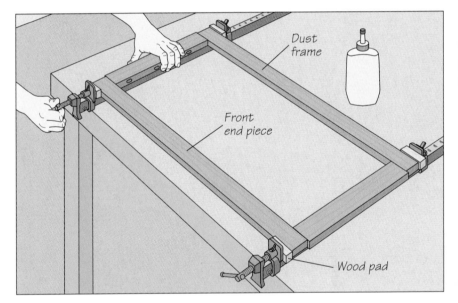

Dust frame

Front end piece

Wood pad

2 Making and gluing up the dust frames

Cut the pieces of the dust frames to length and drill elongated screw holes in the end boards; to allow for wood movement, the holes should be longer and wider than the shanks of the fasteners you will use to attach the frames to the carcase sides. Sand any frame surfaces that will be difficult to reach after glue up. Cut a plate joint *(photo, page 109)* at each corner of the frames, assemble the joints with wood biscuits and glue, then secure them with bar clamps, aligning the bars with the end pieces and protecting the stock with wood pads *(above)*. Make sure the front end piece is recessed by an amount equal to the depth of the dadoes you cut in step 1. When making the dust frame for the two narrower drawers, include the cross rail *(page 106)*.

ASSEMBLING THE CARCASE

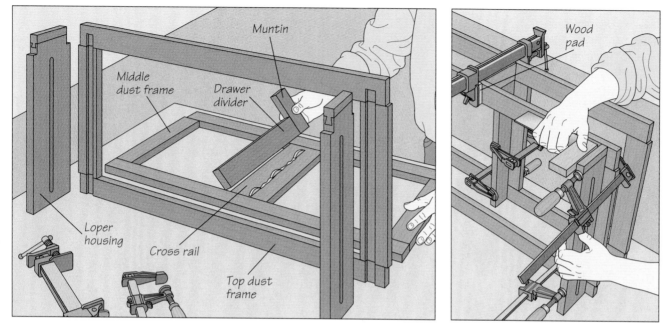

1 Installing the drawer divider and loper housings

Cut the loper housings to size *(page 108)*, using a sliding dovetail to add a piece to the front end of each one to hide the end grain. Then rout the ¼-inch-wide slots in the housings for the loper dowels. Make the L-shaped drawer divider and attach it to the cross rail of the middle dust frame with a biscuit joint *(above, left)*. Cut another biscuit slot into the muntin and a matching slot in the top dust frame above it.

Next, rout grooves into the underside of the top panel and top face of the uppermost dust frame to accommodate the loper housings. Spread glue in the slots and grooves, then fit the dust frames together, using clamps to secure the drawer divider, the loper housings, and the frames in place. Protect the stock with wood pads and use a try square to check that the assembly is square *(above, right)*.

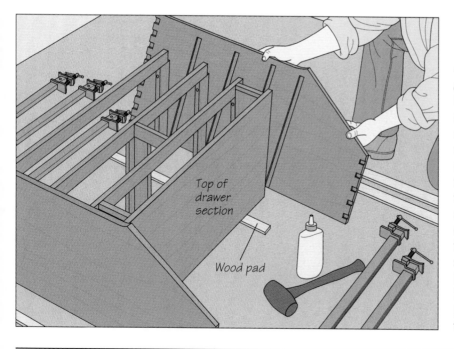

2 Fitting the sides and dust frames together

Working on the shop floor, spread glue along the entire length of the side panel dadoes for the top panel of the drawer unit, but only in the front 2 inches of the dadoes for the dust frames. To allow for wood movement, the remaining length of the dust frames will be attached to the sides with screws. Laying one side panel outside-face down on long wood pads, fit the dust frames into their dadoes and screw them in place. Fit the top panel into its dado, carefully turn the assembly onto its back, and set the other side panel in position *(left)*. Drive the remaining screws to secure the dust frames and side panel.

3 Clamping the assembly

Cut the back panel to fit into the rabbets in the carcase and set it in place; the panel will help keep the assembly square as you tighten the clamps. Protecting the stock with long wood pads, install four clamps across the front of the assembly; align the bars with the dust frames and top panel of the drawer unit. Repeat the process across the back of the carcase *(right)*. To apply pressure to the center of the top panel, place a caul between the clamps with a shim in the middle. Tighten the clamps evenly a little at a time.

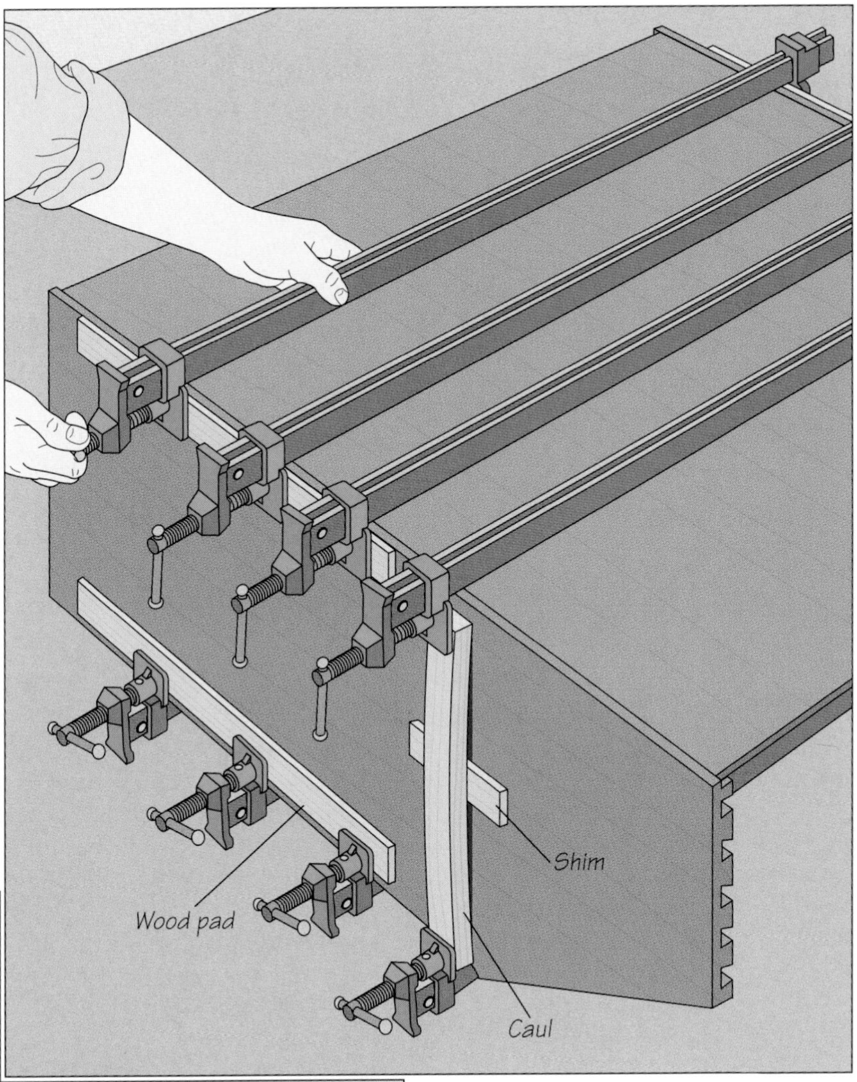

Shim

Wood pad

Caul

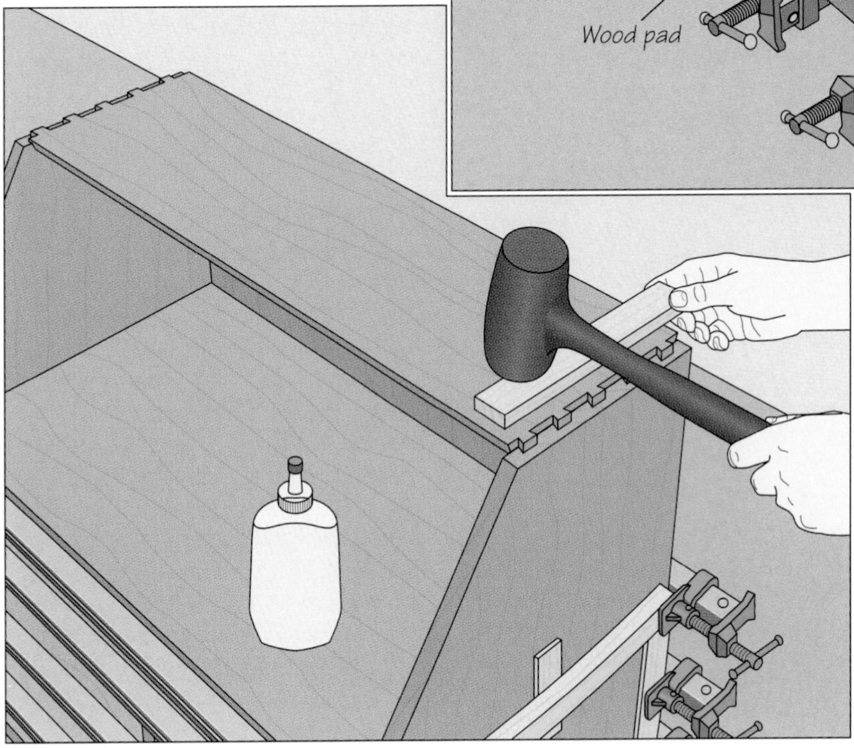

4 Attaching the top and bottom of the desk unit

Test-fit the dovetails joining the top and bottom panels of the desk unit to the sides; correct any overly tight joints by paring away waste wood with a chisel. Then spread glue on the contacting surfaces and tap the panels in place using a dead-blow hammer and a wood block to distribute the pressure *(left)*. The joints should be snug enough to make clamping unnecessary.

5 Installing the back panel

Once the glue has cured, remove the clamps and fix the back panel to the rabbets around its perimeter, driving a finishing nail every 6 inches. For extra rigidity, also nail the panel to the dust frames and top panel of the drawer unit. Use a tape measure to make sure you drive the nails at the correct locations—centered on the dust frames and panel *(right)*.

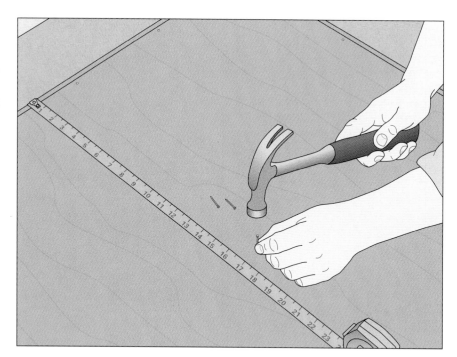

INSTALLING THE LOPERS

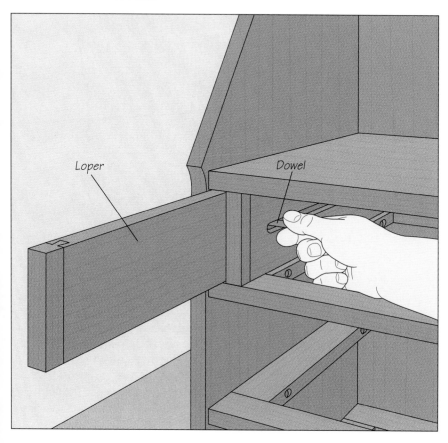

Fitting the lopers in place

Make loper blanks as you did the housings *(page 113)*, gluing a long-grain piece to the front end with a sliding dovetail. Then slide your blanks into their slots between the housings and the side panels, and mark them flush with the front edge of the top panel of the drawer unit; also mark the location of the housing slots on the lopers. Cut the lopers to length and drill a dowel hole into each one in line with the slot outline; locate the hole so the front edge of the fall-front will project about 2 to 3 inches beyond the loper when it is fully extended *(left)*. Cut the dowels 1¼ inches long, then spread glue in the dowel holes. Slide the lopers into their slots and tap the dowels in place.

MAKING THE DRAWERS

The desk unit drawers are assembled with through dovetails, then a false front is glued to the drawer front to conceal the end grain of the tails. The chamfer cut around the perimeter of the false front shown above recalls the traditional practice of beveling the ends and edges of veneered drawer fronts, which prevented the veneer from being torn off when the drawer was opened and closed.

GLUING UP THE DRAWERS

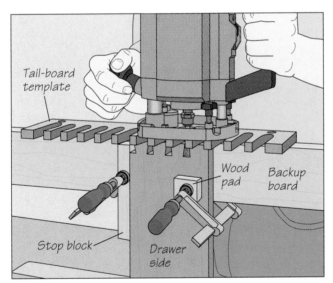

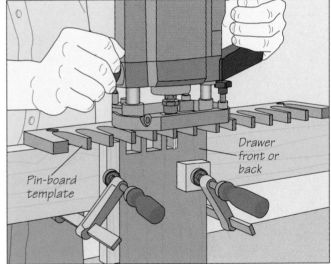

1 Routing the through dovetail joints

Size the drawer parts to fit their openings in the desk unit, then join the boards with dovetails, cutting the pins in the front and back of the drawer, and the tails in the sides. To cut the dovetails with a router and the jig shown above, screw the pin- and tail-board templates to backup boards, then secure one of the tail boards (drawer sides) end up in a bench vise. Protecting the stock with a wood pad, clamp the tail template to the workpiece so the underside of the template is butted against the end of the board. Also clamp a stop block against one edge of the drawer side so the tails at the other end and in the other

drawer sides will match. Install a top-piloted dovetail bit in the router and cut the tails by feeding the tool along the top of the template and moving the bit in and out of the jig's slots *(above, left)*. Keep the bit pilot pressed against the sides of the slot throughout. Repeat to rout the tails at the other end of the board and in the other drawer sides. Then use the completed tails to outline the pins on the drawer fronts and backs. Secure a pin board in the vise, clamp the pin-board template to the board with the slots aligned over the outline, and secure the stop block in place. Rout the pins with a straight bit *(above, right)*.

2 Preparing the drawers for bottom panels

The bottom of each desk unit drawer fits into a groove along the inside of the drawer. Dry-fit the parts together, then clamp the unit securely, protecting the stock with wood pads and aligning the clamp bars with the front and back. Fit a router with a piloted three-wing slotting cutter and mount the tool in a table. Adjust the bit height to cut the groove ¼ inch from the drawer's bottom edge. Set the drawer right side up on the table and, starting at the middle of one side, feed the stock into the cutter against the direction of bit rotation. Keeping the pilot bearing butted against the workpiece, feed the drawer clockwise *(right)*. Continue pivoting the drawer on the table until you return to the starting point. Use veneered plywood for the bottom and cut the panel to fit the opening.

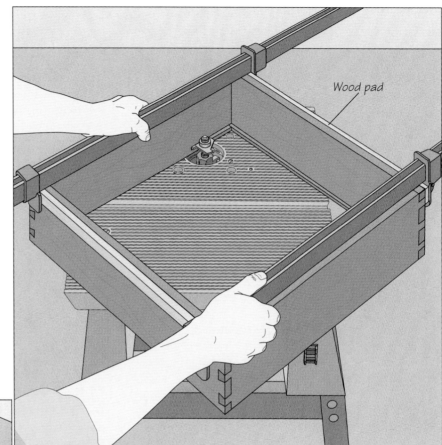

Wood pad

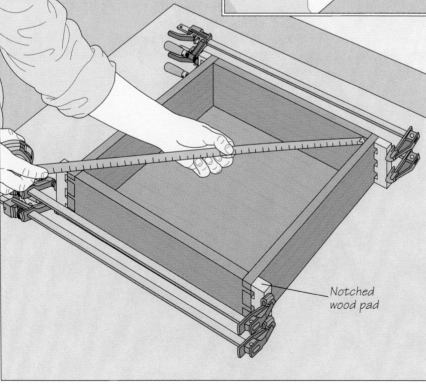

Notched wood pad

3 Gluing and clamping the drawers

For glue up, make four wood pads as long as the height of the drawers and cut small notches in the pads so they only contact the tails. Spread a thin, even layer of glue on all the contacting surfaces, then assemble the drawers and install two bar clamps across the pin boards. Tighten the clamps a little at a time until a small amount of glue squeezes out of the joints. Immediately measure the diagonals between opposite corners *(left)*. The two results should be the same. If not, install another bar clamp across the longer of the two diagonals, setting the clamp jaws on those already in place. Tighten the clamp a little at a time, measuring as you go until the two diagonals are equal.

INSTALLING THE FALSE FRONT

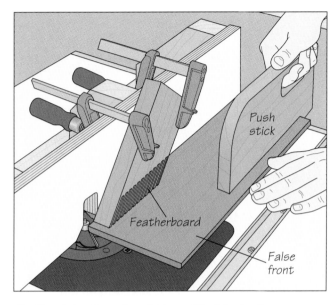

1 Chamfering the ends and edges of the false fronts
Cut the false fronts to fit the drawer openings in the desk unit, subtracting 1/16 inch from the length and width. To chamfer the perimeter of the false fronts, install a piloted 45° chamfering bit in a router and mount the tool in a table. Align the fence with the bit's pilot bearing and adjust the height of the bit to cut all but 3/16 inch of the false front's ends and edges. Clamp two featherboards to the fence, one on each side of the bit, to support the stock. (In the illustration above, the featherboard on the outfeed side of the fence has been removed for clarity.) To reduce tearout, chamfer the ends before the sides. Feed the workpiece across the table with a push stick, using your left hand to press the stock against the fence (above).

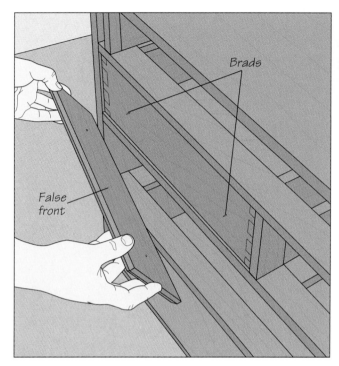

2 Positioning the false fronts
Set each drawer face-up on a work surface and drive two brads into the drawer front, leaving their heads protruding. Make sure the brads are not located where the drawer pull will be installed, then snip off the heads and install the drawer in the desk unit. Carefully position the false front over the drawer (above). Once you are satisfied with the placement, press firmly; the pointed ends of the brads will punch impressions into the back of the false front.

3 Gluing on the false fronts
Remove the drawer and spread a thin layer of glue on the back of the false front. Place the front in position, with the two brads in their impressions. Hold the assembly together, using bar clamps along the top edge of the front and deep-throated C clamps along the bottom edge; protect the stock with wood pads where necessary. Tighten the clamps evenly until there are no gaps between the false front and the drawer (right).

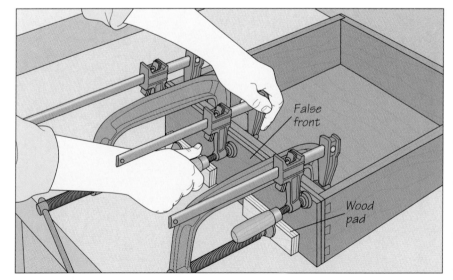

BUILDING THE PIGEONHOLE UNIT

The pigeonhole unit is made to fit between the tops of the desk and drawer sections of the secretary. Molding can be tacked in place to hide the gap between the two carcases, as shown at left. You can also omit the molding, leaving the pigeonhole unit removable.

MAKING THE UNIT

1 Rough-cutting the arches

Referring to the anatomy illustration of the pigeonhole unit *(page 108)*, outline the shape of the arches on a piece of ¾-inch plywood, cut it out, and smooth the edges to fashion a template that you will use to make a routing jig *(step 2)*. Before assembling the jig, use the template to outline six copies of the shape on your arch stock. Cut out the arches to within ⅛ inch of your cutting lines using the band saw. To keep the blade from binding in the kerfs, make a series of release cuts through the waste, stopping ⅛ inch from the lines. Then saw along the waste side of the lines, feeding the workpiece with both hands *(right)*. Make sure that neither hand is in line with the blade.

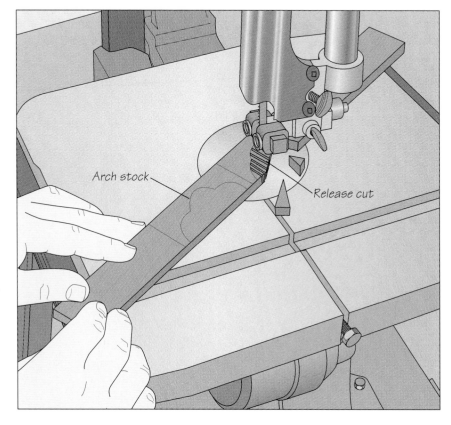

Arch stock

Release cut

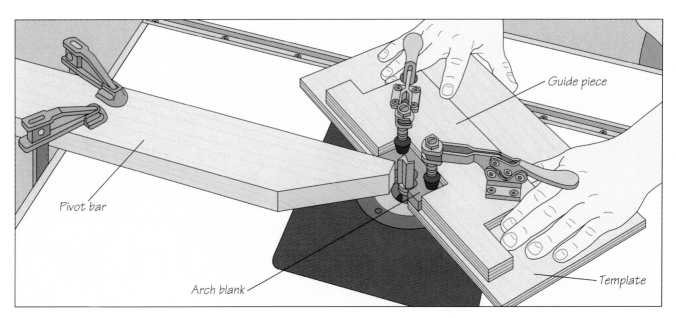

2 Shaping the arches

To complete the routing jig, prepare a guide piece with a notch to fit the arch blanks you cut in step 1, and fasten it to the template, centering the notch over the arch outline. Screw two toggle clamps to the guide piece and secure the first blank to the jig. Next, install a top-piloted flush-cutting bit in your router, mount the tool in a table, and adjust the bit height so the pilot bearing will ride against the template. To complete the setup, clamp a picket-shaped pivot bar to the table in line with, and almost touching, the bit. To trim the arches to final shape, hold the jig with both hands and press the template at one end of the arch pattern against the pivot bar. Then pivot the jig and blank into the bit. Once the template contacts the pilot bearing, shape the arch by guiding the cutter along it, starting with the bearing pressed against one end of the pattern, riding it along the template, and stopping when it contacts the opposite end *(above)*.

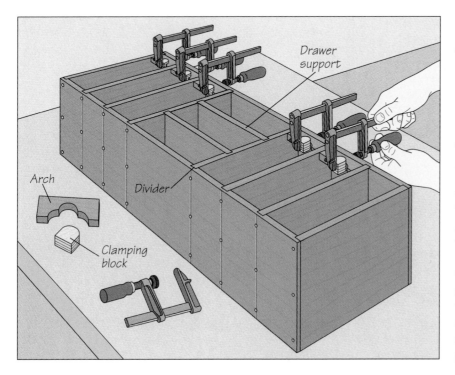

3 Gluing up the unit

Cut the parts of the pigeonhole unit to size and prepare them for assembly. In the top and bottom, cut dadoes for the dividers and rabbets for the sides; in the middle two dividers, cut dadoes for the drawer supports. Spread glue on the contacting surfaces and clamp the assembly securely; reinforce the joints with finishing nails. Make six curved clamping blocks to fit in the middle curves of the arches. When the unit is ready, remove the clamps and apply adhesive to the straight edges of the arches, then clamp them to the unit, using the curved clamping blocks to distribute the pressure squarely *(left)*. Referring to the anatomy *(page 108)*, make three drawers for the pigeonhole unit, rabbeting the drawer fronts for the sides and dadoing the sides for the backs. Attach a pull to each drawer front.

MAKING THE FALL-FRONT

Once the frame for the fall-front has been assembled and hinged to the desk unit, the leather top can be glued to the inside face. The leather should be cut slightly larger than the recess. Use contact cement, hide glue, or thick wallpaper paste to attach the material to the surface. Trim it to size with a craft knife, then smooth it down with a hand roller, as shown at left. The leather should be treated with glycerine saddle soap once a year.

PREPARING THE FRAME

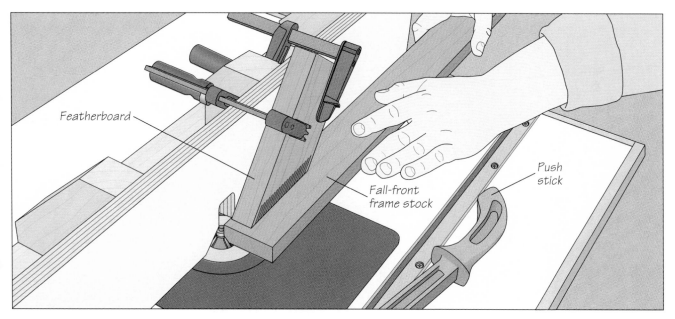

1 Shaping the frame edges

Cut the four frame pieces for the fall-front from a single board. But before making these cuts, shape one edge of the board. Install a piloted 45° chamfering bit in your router, mount the tool in a table, and adjust the height of the bit so it will cut a ⅜-inch-wide bevel into the stock. Align the fence with the bit pilot bearing and clamp two featherboards to the fence, one on each side of the bit, to support the workpiece. Feed the stock face down (above), finishing the pass with a push stick. (In the illustration, the featherboard on the outfeed side of the fence has been removed for clarity.)

2 Preparing the frame for the panel

The fall-front panel sits in a groove cut around the inside edges of the frame. Install a piloted three-wing slotting cutter in the router and align the fence with the bit's pilot bearing. Adjust the bit height so the top edge of the cutter is centered on the edge of the stock. Since the groove will have to accommodate both the panel and the veneer glued to it, you will need at least two passes to rout a sufficiently wide groove. Feed the stock as in step 1, riding the unchamfered edge along the fence; finish the pass with a push stick. Then turn over the workpiece and repeat to widen the groove *(right)*. Now, cut the four frame pieces to length, mitering the ends. Once the veneered panel is ready, the frame will be assembled using plate joints. (The finished frame, along with the veneered panel, is shown on page 104.)

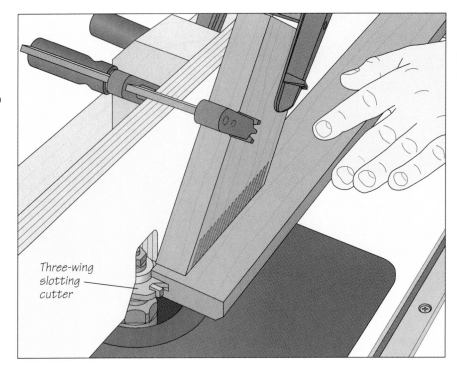

Three-wing slotting cutter

A VARIETY OF VENEERED PANELS

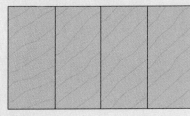

Slip match
Often used to dramatic effect; reduces distortion caused by light refraction problems when book-matching

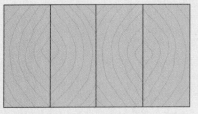

Book match
A repeating pattern in which adjoining sheets of veneer appear to radiate from the joint between them, like the pages of an open book

Herringbone
Veneer figure runs diagonally off each sheet, creating a zigzag effect

End-to-end
A mirror-image pattern featuring flat-cut veneers with prominent landscape figure

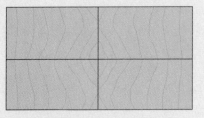

Butt-and-book match
Commonly used with butt, crotch, and stump veneers to create an unfolding, circular effect

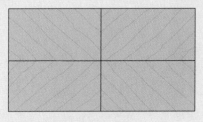

Reverse-diamond match
Features four sheets of veneer that appear to converge at the center

MAKING THE VENEERED PANEL

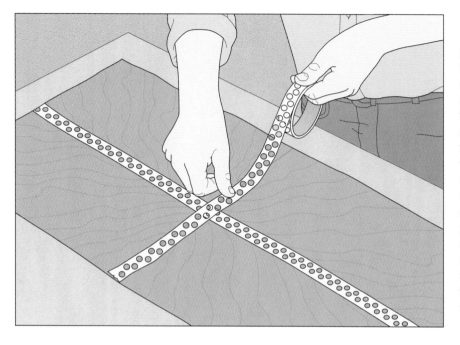

1 Creating the veneer pattern
Cover the outside face of the full-front panel with veneer. You can buy ready-matched sheets and glue them down as-is or make your own match, referring to one of the patterns illustrated on page 122; the secretary featured in this chapter uses a butt-and-book match. To apply more than one sheet of veneer to a panel face with a veneer press *(page 124)*, tape the sheets together and glue them down as a unit. Start by aligning the sheets edge to edge on a work surface, good-side up, to produce a visually interesting pattern. The combined length and width of the veneer should equal the dimensions of the panel. Once you have a satisfactory arrangement, tape the sheets together using veneer tape *(left)*.

2 Setting up a vacuum press
Featuring a sealed vacuum bag and a 5-cfm (cubic feet per minute) vacuum pump, the press shown in step 3 can exert pressure greater than 1,000 pounds per square foot. The press works by withdrawing most of the air from the bag; the resulting outside air pressure secures the veneer. To set up the press, cut the platen and caul to the same size as your substrate panel *(right)*. The platen should be made from medium-density fiberboard or particleboard at least ¾ inch thick. Cut the caul from any type of manufactured board (other than plywood) at least ½ inch thick. To prepare the platen, round over its corners to avoid tearing the bag, then cut a grid of grooves ⅛ inch deep and wide across its surface, spaced 4 to 6 inches apart. Finally, bore a ⅝-inch hole 2 inches from one end of the platen and centered between its edges. Slip the sleeve supplied with the press into the hole. The sleeve will ensure a tight connection with the vacuum hose.

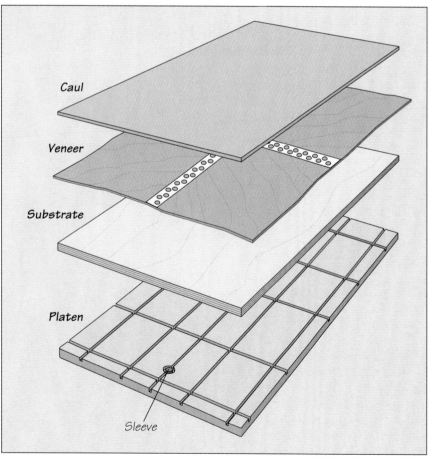

Caul

Veneer

Substrate

Platen

Sleeve

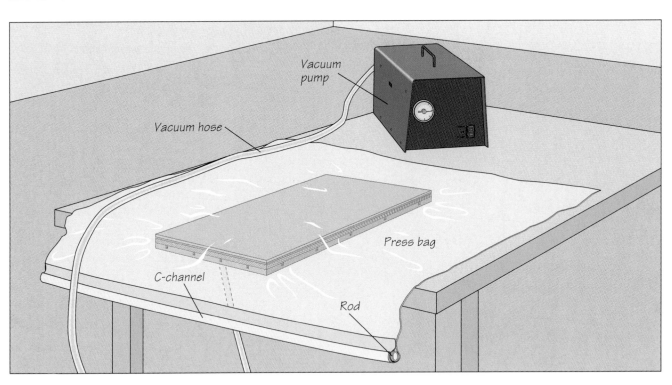

3 Veneering the panel

Use the vacuum press to glue the veneer down to the panel, following the manufacturer's instructions. For the model shown, insert the hose into the nipple in the bottom of the press bag. Then place the platen in the bag and slide the nipple into the platen sleeve. Set the substrate panel on a work surface, apply the glue, and lay the veneer tape-side up on the substrate. Place a piece of wax paper over the veneer, rest the caul on top, and place the assembly atop the platen. Seal the bag, turn on the pump and leave the assembly under pressure for the recommended length of time *(above)*. Most vacuum presses will automatically shut off when the appropriate pressure has been reached.

4 Assembling the fall-front

Once the veneer has been secured, remove the tape and gently sand surfaces that will be difficult to reach after the frame is glued together. Ready the frame pieces for plate joints *(page 109)*, applying the glue and wood biscuits at the mitered end of the boards. Do not insert any adhesive in the panel grooves; the panel must be free to move. To prevent the wood biscuits from expanding before everything is put together, assemble the frame as quickly as possible, fitting the frames pieces to the panel *(right)*. With wood pads protecting the frame, secure the plate joints with bar clamps.

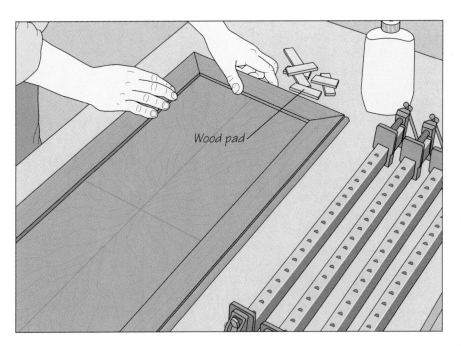

VENEER PRESS

Made from plywood, hardwood, and six 9-inch-long press screws, the inexpensive shop-built veneer press shown below will work as well as a commercial model. The dimensions provided in the illustration will yield a press capable of veneering panels up to 16 by 29½ inches.

Start by cutting the rails and stiles from hardwood. Bore three equidistant holes through the middle of each top rail, sized slightly larger than the diameter of the press screw collars you will be using. Next, join the rails and stiles into two rectangular frames.

The press in the illustration is assembled with open mortise-and-tenon joints *(inset)*, but through dovetails can also be used. Whichever joinery method you use, reinforce each joint with glue and three screws.

Now cut the pieces for the base and caul to size. Both are made from two pieces of ¾-inch plywood face-glued and screwed together. To assemble the press, set the two frames on their sides on a work surface and screw the base to the bottom rails, driving the fasteners from the bottom of the rails. Attach the press screws to the top rails by removing the swivel heads and

collars, then tapping the collars into the holes in the top rails from underneath. Slip the threaded sections into the collars and reattach them to the swivel heads.

To use the press, apply the glue and lay the veneer tape-side up on the substrate. Set the panel on the base of the press, veneered-face down with a strip of wax paper between the veneer and the base. Starting in the middle of the panel to prevent adhesive from becoming trapped, tighten the press clamps one at a time until a thin glue bead squeezes out from under the panel.

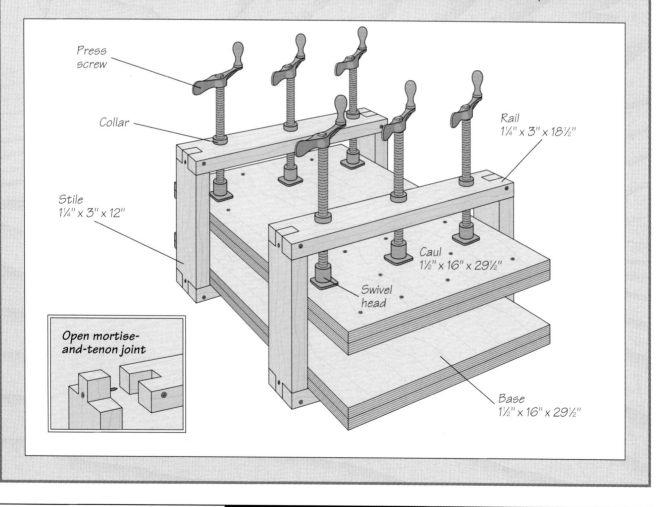

Press screw

Collar

Stile
1¼" x 3" x 12"

Rail
1¼" x 3" x 18½"

Caul
1½" x 16" x 29½"

Swivel head

Base
1½" x 16" x 29½"

Open mortise-and-tenon joint

ATTACHING THE FALL-FRONT TO THE DESK UNIT

Top frame
piece of
fall-front

Hinge mortise

Carving
gouge

Rabbet

Top of
desk
unit

Top of
drawer
section

Chisel

Loper

1 Making the hinge mortises
Use your table saw to cut a ⅜-inch-wide rabbet *(page 59)* along the sides of the frame. Begin with a shallow depth of cut, increasing the depth by ⅛ inch with each pass until the fall-front's bottom edge is 1/16 inch above the top of the drawer unit when the fall-front is in position. Once you are satisfied with the fit, lay the fall-front veneer-face down on the lopers and butt the bottom edge against the top of the drawer section. Position and outline the three hinges on the pieces—one in the middle and one each near the sides—centering the hinge pin on the seam between the fall-front and the carcase. To cut the hinge mortises, install a ⅛-inch straight bit in your router, set the cutting depth to the hinge leaf thickness, and cut out the waste inside the outline. Use a chisel, a carving gouge, and a wooden mallet to pare to the line *(left)*. Test-fit the hinges in their mortises and use the chisel to deepen or widen any of the recesses, if necessary.

2 Attaching the fall-front to the desk unit
Set the hinges in their mortises in the desk unit and mark the screw holes, then drill pilot holes and screw the hinge leaves in place, leaving the fasteners a little loose. Mark the drilling depth on the drill bit by wrapping a strip of masking tape around it. Next, extend the lopers and set the fall-front in position, slipping the free hinge leaves into their mortises. Mark the screw holes, drill pilot holes, and screw the hinges to the fall-front, then finish tightening all the screws *(right)*. If you are using brass screws, be careful not to overtighten them or they will break. It is a good idea to drive in a standard wood screw first to tap the pilot hole.

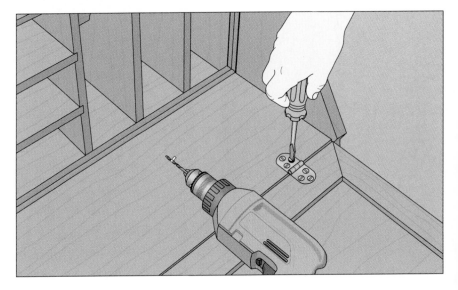

INSTALLING THE FALL-FRONT LOCK

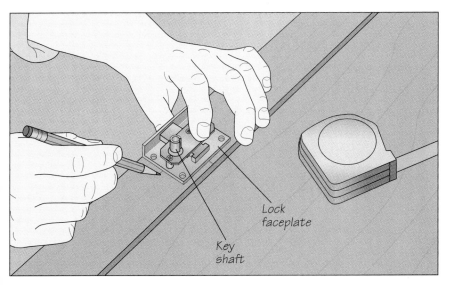

Lock
faceplate

Key
shaft

1 Outlining the lock faceplate
Open the fall-front to its down position and place the lock face down on the top frame piece so the key shaft will be centered between the sides; the lock should also be flush with the top edge of the panel. If the key shaft is off-center, as is the case with the lock shown, you will need to use a tape measure and a try square to mark the middle of the fall-front and align the key shaft with it *(left)*. Drill the hole for the key shaft and insert the shaft through the hole. Once the lock is properly positioned, trace the outline of the lock faceplate, then extend the lines onto the top edge of the fall-front.

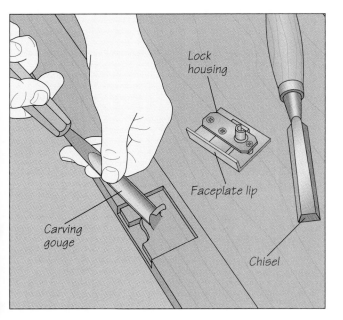

Lock
housing

Faceplate lip

Carving
gouge

Chisel

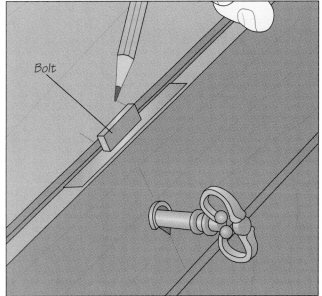

Bolt

2 Routing the lock mortise
Start by using a chisel to cut a shallow mortise for the faceplate lip in the top edge of the fall-front. Next, install a straight bit in your router, set the cutting depth to the faceplate thickness, and cut a mortise within the marked outline. Use the chisel to square the corners and pare to the line. To cut the mortise for the lock housing, measure the distance between the edges of the faceplate and the housing, and transfer your measurement to the mortise. Then use a carving gouge to cut the final mortise *(above)*. Test-fit the lock in the cavity and use the chisel or gouge to deepen or widen any of the mortises, if necessary. Finally, screw the lock in place.

3 Installing the strike plate
Fit the key into the lock. To locate the strike plate for the bolt, turn the key to extend the bolt and use a pencil to coat the end of the bolt with graphite. Retract the bolt and swing the fall-front to the closed position. Extend the bolt against the underside of the carcase top to mark its location. Also extend the bolt against the edge of the top panel and mark its sides on the top *(above)*. Position the strike plate on the carcase top, centering its opening on the pencil marks. Outline the plate, then cut a shallow recess for it and a deeper mortise for the bolt. Finally, mark the plate's screw holes, bore a pilot hole at each mark, and fasten the plate in position.

The bottom of the secretary's desk unit sits on a base supported by bracket feet at each corner. The bottom edges of the carcase are concealed by molding, which is attached to the base, but not glued to the carcase. This allows the panels of the desk unit to move with changes in humidity without damaging the molding.

MAKING AND INSTALLING THE BASE

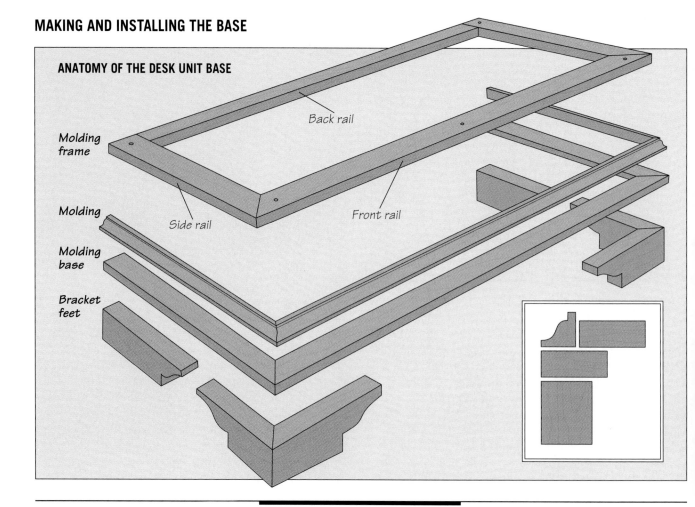

ANATOMY OF THE DESK UNIT BASE

Molding
frame

Molding

Molding
base

Bracket
feet

Back rail

Side rail

Front rail

1 Routing the molding

Cut a board longer and wider than you will need for the three pieces of molding. Install a Roman ogee bit *(inset)* in your router and mount the tool in a table. Align the bit's pilot bearing with the fence and adjust the cutting height to leave a flat lip no more than ¼ inch thick on the edge of the stock above the molding. Mount two featherboards on the fence and one on the table to secure the workpiece. (In this illustration, the featherboard on the outfeed side of the fence has been removed for clarity.) Turn on the tool and feed the stock *(right)*. To complete the pass, move to the outfeed side of the table and pull the stock through the end of the cut. Make several passes, increasing the width of cut ⅛ inch at a time. Rip the molding strips from the board on your table saw, then cut them to length, mitering both ends of the front piece and the front end of the side pieces.

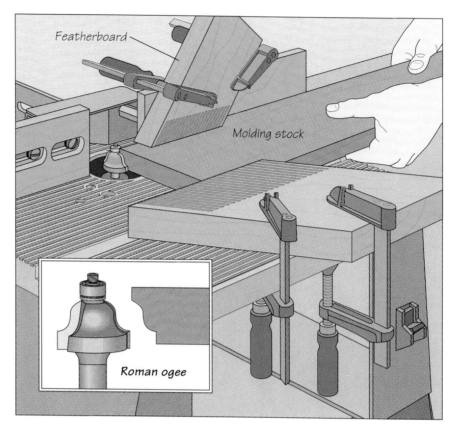

Featherboard

Molding stock

Roman ogee

2 Gluing up the base

Cut the rails of the molding frame and molding base to length, mitering both ends of the front pieces and the front end of the side pieces; omit the back rail for the base. Join the corners of the frames with plate joints *(page 109)* and clamp them as you did the dust frames *(page 112)*. Next, glue the molding base to the underside of the frame so the sides of the base extend beyond the frame by about 1 inch. Then cut the bracket feet on your band saw. Spread glue on the contacting surfaces between the molding pieces, the bracket feet, and the molding base, then fit the pieces together and clamp the assembly, protecting the stock with wood pads *(left)*. Once the adhesive has cured, remove the clamps and attach the base to the desk unit by screwing the molding frame to the carcase through elongated screw holes.

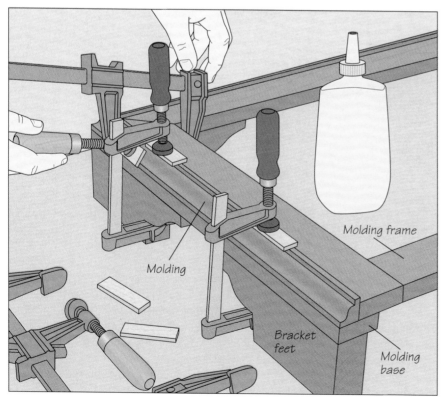

Molding frame

Molding

Bracket feet

Molding base

MAKING THE BOOKCASE

Adjustable shelves give the book-case section of the secretary greater flexibility, enabling you to adapt to changing needs and organize space most efficiently. The solid brass shelf supports shown at right can be slipped into any of the sleeves along the side panels, permitting the shelves to be mounted at any height in the bookcase.

PREPARING THE SIDE PANELS FOR ADJUSTABLE SHELVING

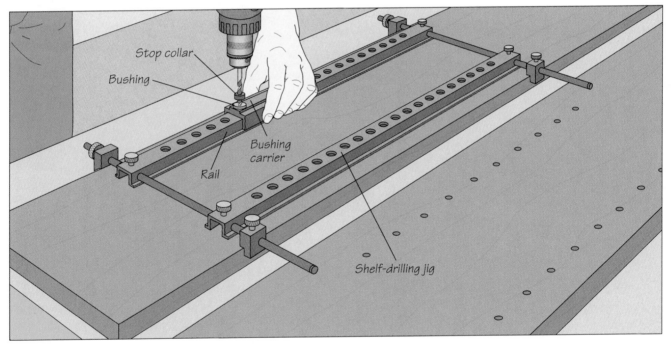

Stop collar

Bushing

Bushing carrier

Rail

Shelf-drilling jig

1 Drilling holes for shelf supports
Cut the side panels of the bookcase to width and length, then set them inside-face up on a work surface. The commercial jig shown above enables you to bore two parallel rows of holes in the side panels at 1-inch intervals and ensures that corresponding holes will be perfectly aligned. Clamp the jig to the edges of one panel; the holes can be any distance from the panel edges, but about 2 inches in would be best for the secretary. Fit an electric drill with a bit the same diameter as the sleeves

and install a stop collar to mark the drilling depth equal to the sleeve length. Starting at either end of one of the jig's rails, place the appropriate bushing in the first hole of the bushing carrier. (The bushing keeps the bit perfectly square to the work-piece.) Holding the drill and carrier, bore the hole. Drill a series of evenly spaced holes along both rails. Remove the jig and repeat for the other side panel, carefully positioning the jig so that the holes will be aligned with those in the first panel.

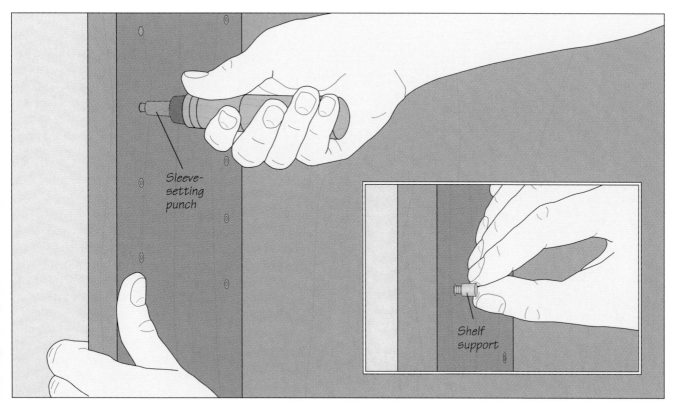

Sleeve-
setting
punch

Shelf
support

2 Mounting the sleeves and supports

To install the sleeves without damaging them, use a sleeve-setting punch. Place a sleeve on the end of the punch and push it firmly into one of the holes in a side panel *(above)*. Insert a sleeve into each hole you drilled. Once you have installed all the sleeves, insert shelf supports into the sleeves at each shelf location *(inset)*.

SHOP TIP

**A shop-made
shelf-drilling jig**
The T-shaped jig shown here will enable you to drill a row of evenly spaced holes as accurately as with a commercial jig. Make the jig from 1-by-3 stock, being careful to screw the fence and arm together at a perfect 90° angle. Mark a line down the middle of the arm and drill holes at 2-inch intervals along it with the same bit you would use for the sleeves. To use the jig, clamp it to the side panel with the fence butted against either end of the panel and the marked centerline 2 inches in from its edge. Fit your drill bit with a stop collar, bore the holes, and reposition the jig for each new row.

ASSEMBLING THE CARCASE

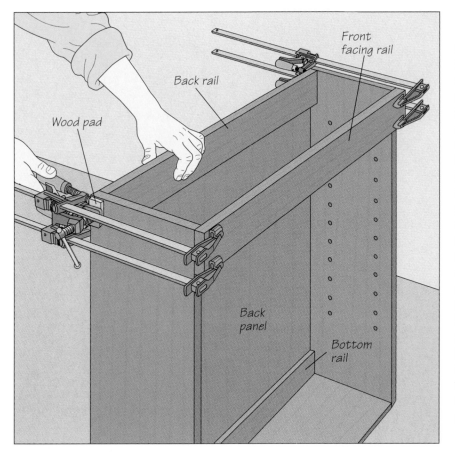

Back rail

Front facing rail

Wood pad

Back panel

Bottom rail

1 Gluing up the sides, bottom, and rails
Cut the remaining pieces of the book-case carcase to size—the bottom, the rails, and the back panel. Next, saw a rabbet along the back edges of the sides and bottom for the back panel. Cut blind tenons at both ends of the back rail *(page 59)* and drill a matching mortise *(page 58)* on the inside face of each side panel. With a plate joiner, make slots for biscuits in the front and bottom rails, and mating ones in the sides. Use half-blind dovetails *(page 109)* to join the sides to the bottom of the bookcase, cutting the pins in the sides and the tails in the bottom. Then spread glue on the contacting surfaces of all the pieces, inserting wood biscuits where appropriate, and fit them together. Protecting the stock with wood pads, install two bar clamps across each side, positioning the clamp jaws on the front and back rails, then install two more clamps across the back and bottom rails. Tighten the clamps evenly *(left)* until a thin glue bead squeezes out of the joints. Finally, nail the back panel *(page 115)* in place.

2 Routing a groove for the top panel
To attach the top panel to the book-case using wood buttons, as shown in this section, you will need to rout a groove for the buttons along the top of the carcase. Fit your router with a pilot-ed three-wing slotting cutter and set the tool's cutting depth to locate the groove about ½ inch below the top edge of the carcase. Starting near one corner, guide the router along the top edge *(right)*. Move the tool in a clockwise direction, keeping the base plate flat and the bit's pilot bearing pressed against the stock.

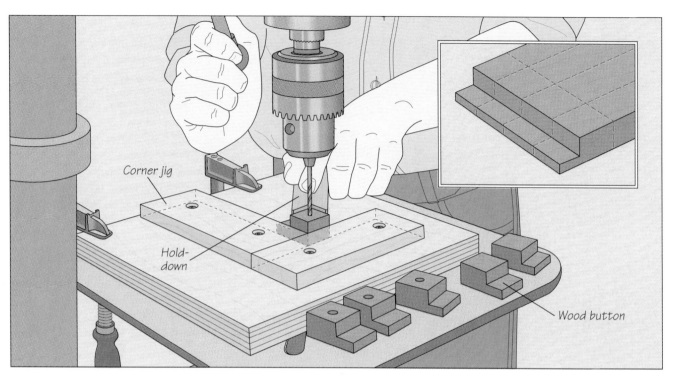

3 Making the buttons

You will need to place a wood button every 6 inches along the top edge of the carcase. Cut several 1-by-1¾-inch buttons from a single board; make the thickness of the stock equal to the gap between the bottom of the groove and the top edge of the carcase, less ⅟₁₆ inch. Cut a rabbet to fit the groove at each end of the board, then rip the board into 1-inch strips on your band saw and cut off the buttons about 1¾ inches from the ends *(inset)*. To make holes in the buttons for installation, use an L-shaped corner jig fashioned from a scrap of ¾-inch plywood and two pieces of wood. Clamp the jig to your drill press table and steady the buttons with a hold-down made from scrap wood. Drill through the centers on the unrabbeted portions of the buttons *(above)*.

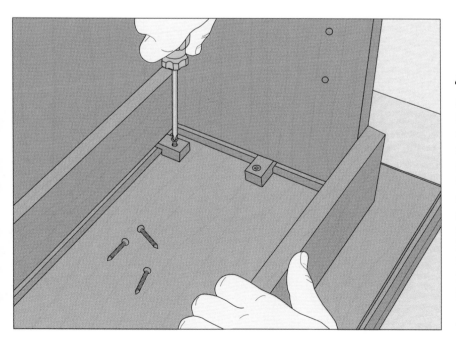

4 Attaching the top

Cut the bookcase top to size, then shape its ends and edges on a router table *(page 118)*, using a decorative molding bit. Set the top outside-face down on a work surface and position the carcase on top. Fit the rabbeted end of a wood button into the groove in one of the side panels and insert another into the groove in the back rail about 6 inches away. Drill a pilot hole through the hole in the button and into the top, then screw the buttons in place *(left)*, leaving a ⅛-inch gap between the lipped ends of the buttons and the bottom of the groove. Install the remaining buttons, spacing them every 6 inches.

MAKING AND INSTALLING CROWN MOLDING

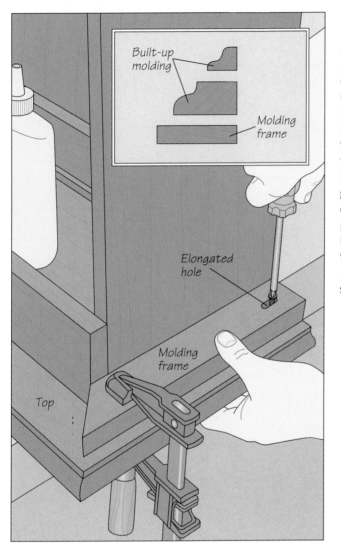

Built-up molding

Molding frame

Elongated hole

Molding frame

Top

1 Making the molding and attaching the frame
Fixed to the underside of the bookcase top and flush against the carcase, the crown molding consists of three layers *(inset)*. Cut the molding frame pieces to length, mitering both ends of the front piece and the front end of each side piece. Create the built-up molding on the router table as you did the base molding *(page 129)*, using two different ogee bits for the narrow and wider pieces. Cut the molding to length, mitering the pieces as you did the frame. Start by installing the molding frame. For the side pieces, drill an elongated hole through each board near the straight end; to allow for wood movement, spread glue on only the first 2 inches of the top face at the mitered end. Now, set the bookcase top-down on a work surface and position one side piece on the underside of the top. Install a bar clamp to secure the mitered end and drive a wood screw through the elongated hole and into the top to fix the back end *(left)*. Repeat for the other side, then install the front piece spreading glue along its entire length.

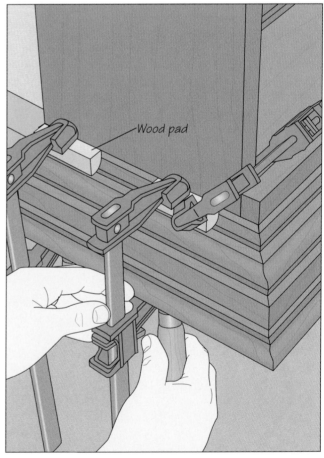

Wood pad

2 Applying the molding
The crown molding is fastened to the bookcase in two steps: The wider strips are attached first, followed by the narrower pieces on top. Spread a thin layer of glue on the bottom face of the wider strips, taking care not to get any glue on the edges since the molding should only be fixed to the molding frame, and not to the carcase. Set the strips on the molding frame, edges flush against the bookcase, making sure that the mitered ends butt together cleanly before clamping the molding in place. Once the adhesive has cured, remove the clamps and repeat the process for the narrower molding strips *(right)*. Cutting wood pads with convex curves matching the concave profile of the molding will not only protect the stock, but also help distribute clamping pressure evenly.

MAKING THE DOORS

An escutcheon is fastened to one of the doors of the bookcase shown at left. On this piece, the key and escutcheons are purely decorative. The doors are actually held shut by spring-loaded catches installed on the inside faces of the stiles near the bottom of the doors.

MAKING FRAME-AND-PANEL DOORS

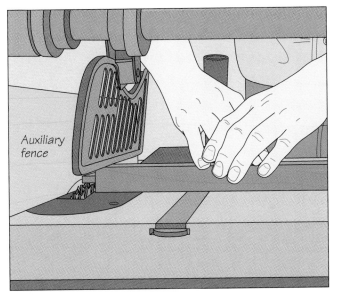

Auxiliary fence

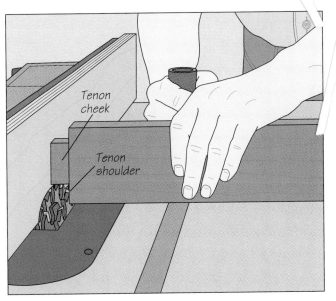

Tenon cheek

Tenon shoulder

1 Cutting the tenon in the rails
Start making the frame-and-panel doors of the bookcase by cutting blind tenons at the ends of all the rails. To do the job on your table saw, install a dado head slightly wider than the tenon length. Attach an auxiliary wood fence and notch it by raising the dado head into it. Set the width of cut equal to the tenon length and adjust the cutting height to about one-third the thickness of the stock. Holding the rail flush against the miter gauge and the fence, feed the stock face-down into the blades to cut one tenon cheek. Turn the board over and make the same cut on the other side. Check for fit

in a test mortise *(step 4)*, then repeat the process on the other end of the board and on the other rails *(above, left)*. To cut the tenon shoulders, set the cutting height at about ½ inch. Then, with the rail face flush against the miter gauge and the end butted against the fence, feed the workpiece into the blades. Turn the rail over and repeat the cut on the other side *(above, right)*. Cut the rest of the tenon shoulders the same way. Fashion integrated molding on the inside edges of the door frames on a router table *(page 129)* using a piloted molding bit.

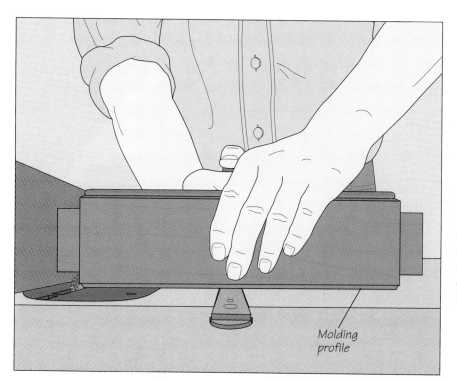

2 Preparing the rails for glue up

The corners of the tenon shoulders must be mitered to mate properly with the stiles. Remove the auxiliary fence from the table saw fence and install a crosscut or combination blade. Set the blade angle to 45°, make a test cut in a scrap board, and check the result with a combination square. Adjust the fence position and blade height so the cut is as wide and deep as the width of the edge molding. (The blade teeth should just protrude beyond the tenon shoulder.) To make the cuts, hold the piece flush against the fence and miter gauge as you feed it edge down into the blade. Repeat the cuts on the ends of each molded edge of the remaining rails *(left)*.

Molding profile

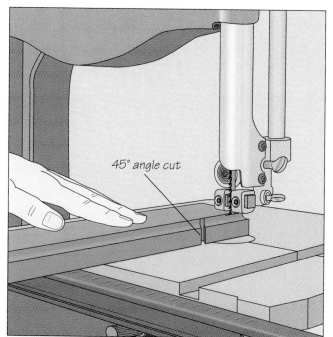

45° angle cut

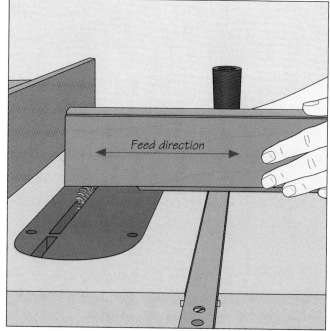

Feed direction

3 Notching the stiles

Leave the table saw blade angled at 45°, measure the width of each rail, and mark a line on the molded edge of its mating stile a corresponding distance from the end. Cut into the molded edge at the line, making certain that the cut will not mar the face of the stile. Slice off most of the strip of molding between the 45° cut and each end of the stile with a band saw *(above, left)*. Smooth the cut edge using the table saw. Leaving the rip fence in place, hold the stile flush against the miter gauge, and slide the stock back and forth across the blade *(above, right)*. Repeat the process for all the stiles.

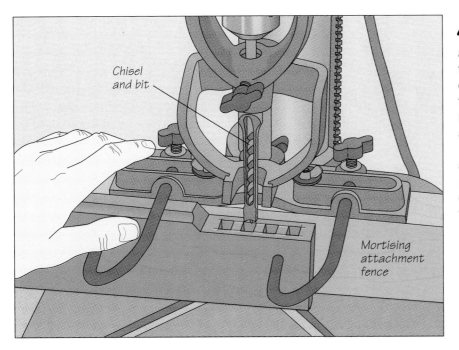

4 Cutting mortises in the stiles

Use one of the tenons you cut in step 1 as a guide to outlining the mortises on the edges of the stiles. To make the job easier, clamp all the stiles together face to face with their ends aligned. Install a mortising attachment on your drill press and clamp one stile to the fence, centering the mortise outline under the chisel and bit. Make the drilling depth $\frac{1}{16}$ inch more than the tenon length; make a cut at each end of the mortise before boring out the waste in between *(left)*. Repeat the procedure to cut the remaining mortises.

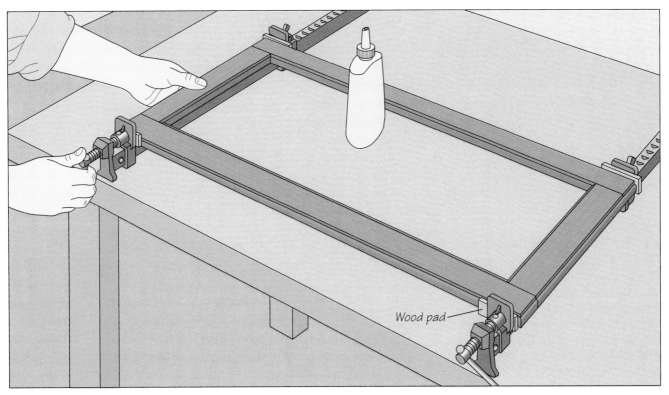

5 Gluing up the doors

Test-assemble the doors and use a chisel to pare away some wood from any overly tight joint. Once you are satisfied with the fit, sand any surfaces that will be difficult to reach when the doors have been glued up, and spread glue on all the contacting surfaces of the joints. Reassemble the doors and set each one on two bar clamps, aligning the bars with the rails. Using wood pads to protect the stock, tighten the clamps *(above)* until a thin glue bead squeezes out of the joints.

INSTALLING THE DOORS

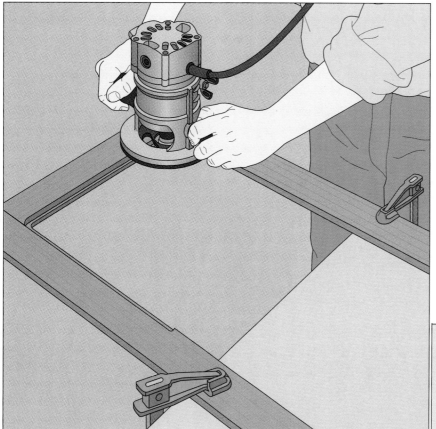

1 Preparing the doors for glass

Glass panels lie in rabbets and are held in place by thin strips of molding. Clamp one door frame to a work surface, then install a piloted ⅜-inch rabbeting bit in your router and set the depth of cut to the combined thickness of the glass and the molding. Hold the tool firmly with both hands while resting the base plate on the frame near one corner, then guide the bit into the inside edge of the door. Move the router clockwise along the edges *(left)*, keeping the pilot bearing pressed against the stock. Square the corners with a chisel and a wooden mallet. Repeat for the second door.

2 Making the molding

Cut a board longer than you will need for the molding, then install a ½-inch cove bit in your router and mount the tool in a table. Align the bit bearing with the fence and adjust the cutter height to shape the bottom corner of the stock. Mount a featherboard on the table in line with the bit to secure the stock during the cut. Turn on the tool and feed the stock, finishing the pass with a push stick. Shape the other edge of the board the same way *(right)*. Rip the molding from the stock on the table saw and cut the molding to length, mitering the ends at 45°. Cut and fit one piece at a time.

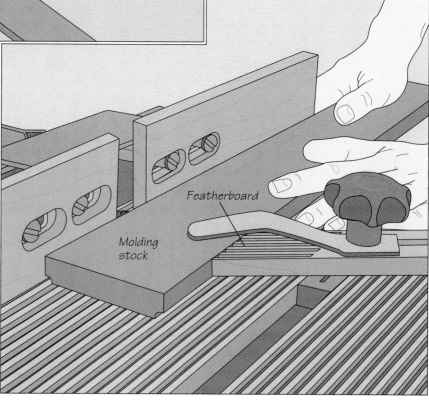

Featherboard

Molding stock

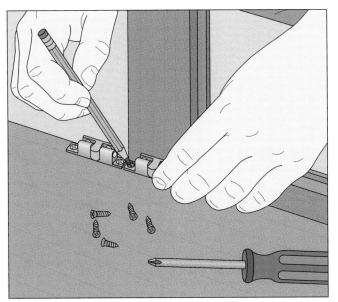

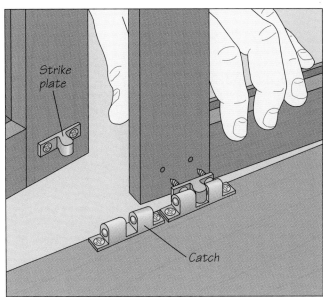

Strike plate

Catch

3 Installing the door catches

Before installing the glass, mount the doors on the bookcase, attaching them with hinges the same way you fastened the fall-front to the desk unit *(page 126)*. It is easier to install the door catches without the glass in place. The ball catches shown above feature a catch fastened to the bottom panel of the bookcase and a strike plate screwed to the inside face of the door stiles; two spring-loaded balls in the catch capture the strike plate when the door is closed. Assemble the catches, hold one

in position against its door stile, then move it toward the back panel by 1/32 inch and mark the screw holes. Drill a pilot hole at each mark and screw the catch in place. Repeat the marking *(above, left)* and fastening process for the other catch. To install the strike plate, insert its screws, engage it with the catch, and close the door; the tips of the screws will mark impressions in the door stile. Drill a pilot hole at each mark and fasten the strike plate to the door. Repeat for the other plate *(above, right)*.

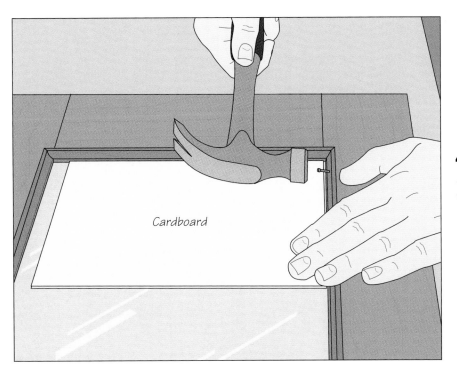

Cardboard

4 Securing the glass

Unscrew the doors from the bookcase and set one door inside face up on a work surface. Set a drop of clear glazing compound every few inches along the rabbet in the door frame to prevent the glass from rattling. Set the glass and the molding in place and, starting 2 inches from the corners, drill pilot holes at 6-inch intervals through the molding and into the frame. Tack down the molding with brads, using a piece of cardboard to protect the glass from the hammer *(left)*. To finish off the secretary, reinstall the doors.

GLOSSARY

A-B-C-D

Adze: An ax-like tool with a curved blade used to carve out concave surfaces, such as chair seats.

Auxiliary fence: A wooden attachment screwed to the rip fence of a table saw or other machine, to prevent damage to the metal fence.

Base molding: A decorative frame made from molded stock that supports the bottom of a desk.

Bead: A rounded, convex shape cut in wood, usually for decoration; *see cove*.

Bending form: A jig used to bend steamed wood.

Bookmatching: In veneering, a decorative pattern in which successive veneers cut from the same log are arranged side-by-side so as to mirror each other's image like pages of an open book.

Bow: The curved upper rail of a sack-back Windsor chair.

Brad-point bit: A drill bit featuring a sharpened centerpoint and two cutting spurs on its circumference; produces cleaner holes than a twist bit and does not tend to skate on the surface when starting a hole.

Carcase: A piece of furniture with a box-like construction; made from solid panels.

Caul: Used in veneering or gluing up carcases, a board placed between clamps and the workpiece to distribute clamping pressure.

Chamfer: A bevel cut along the edge of a workpiece.

Cheek: In a mortise-and-tenon joint, that part of the tenon parallel to the wood grain and perpendicular to the shoulder.

Clearance hole: A hole bored in a workpiece to allow free passage of the shank of a screw.

Corner block: A triangular block of wood screwed to an inside corner of a table's leg-and-rail assembly to reinforce and square the joint.

Counterbore: To drill a hole so the head of a screw or bolt will sit below the wood surface and be concealed with a wood plug.

Countersink: To drill a hole so the head of a screw will lie flush with or slightly below the wood surface.

Cove: A concave decorative profile cut in wood, usually along an edge; see *bead*.

Crown or cornice molding: Molding attached to the top of a piece of furniture.

Cutting list: A list of the dimensions of the lumber needed for a specific project.

Dado: A rectangular channel cut into a workpiece.

Dovetailed half-lap joint: Used for joining the top drawer rail of a table to the legs; the half-lap at the end of the rail is cut in a dovetail shape to lock the joint in tension.

Dovetail joint: A method of joinery using interlocking pins and tails; the name derives from the distinctive shape cut into the ends of the joining boards.

Drop-leaf table: A table with a narrow top and hinged leaves that fold down when not in use.

Dust frame: A flat frame used to support desk drawers.

E-F-G-H-I-J

Escutcheon: A metal plate installed around a keyhole for decoration and protection of the surrounding wood.

False front: A piece of wood installed over a drawer front, usually to conceal the end grain of the sides.

Featherboard: A board with thin, flexible fingers or "feathers" along one end, clamped to the fence or table of a stationary tool to hold the workpiece securely.

Fillet: In a rule joint, the short, flat surface at the top of the rounded-over portion of the joint; the pins of the rule-joint hinges are aligned with the fillet.

Finial: An ornament—usually turned or carved—projecting from the upper corners of a piece of furniture.

Fly rail: A short wood piece that swings out from a table side rail to support a drop leaf.

Froe: An L-shaped tool with a beveled blade that is struck by a club to rive, or split, green wood.

Glass-stop molding: Decorative strips of wood used to hold a pane of glass in place in a door.

Green wood: Freshly cut, unseasoned wood.

Half-blind dovetail: Similar to the through dovetail joint, except that the pins are not cut through the entire thickness of the workpiece, thus concealing the end grain of the tail boards.

Inlay: A decorative strip of metal, hardwood or marquetry that is glued in a groove cut into a workpiece.

Kerf: A cut made in wood by a saw blade.

Kickback: The tendency of a workpiece to be thrown back in the direction of the saw operator by a moving blade or cutter on a woodworking machine or tool.

Knuckle joint: A joint consisting of interlocking fingers fixed together by a wooden pin; enables a fly rail to pivot away from a table side rail.

Lamb's tongue: On a pencil-post bed, the shape at the bottom of the octagonal portion of a bedpost.

Loper: On a slant-top desk, a board that slides out of a housing to support the fall-front in the horizontal position.

Mortise-and-tenon joint: A joinery technique in which a projecting tenon on one board fits into a mortise on another.

Mortise: A rectangular, round, or oval hole cut into a piece of wood to receive a matching tenon.

Neoclassicism: An 18th-Century design movement inspired by the esthetic principles of classical Greece and Rome.

Pigeonhole: A framework of small dividers and drawers in a desk; sometimes removable.

Pilot bearing: A cylindrical metal collar either above or below the router bit's cutting edge that rides along the workpiece or a template, guiding the bit during a cut.

Pilot hole: A hole bored into a workpiece to accommodate a nail shaft or the threaded part of a screw; usually slightly smaller than the fastener diameter. The hole guides the fastener and prevents splitting.

Plate joint: A method of joining using oval wafers of compressed wood that fit into slots cut in mating boards.

Pocket hole: An angled hole bored into the face of a workpiece and exiting from its top edge.

Pommel: A rounded shoulder produced on the lathe; serves to separate square and cylindrical sections of a workpiece.

Rabbet: A step-like cut in the edge or end of a board; usually forms part of a joint.

Rail: A board running along the bottom edge of a tabletop to which the legs can be attached; also, the horizontal member of a frame and panel assembly; see *stile*.

Rake angle: The angle at which a chair leg or post deviates from the vertical when viewed from the side of the chair; see *splay angle*.

Reveal: The gap between the outside surfaces of a table rail and the adjoining legs; serves a decorative purpose.

Riving: The technique of splitting wood from a freshly felled log with a sledgehammer and wedges to separate the wood along the fibers.

Rule joint: A pivoting joint commonly used in drop-leaf tables; features mating concave and convex profiles cut into the edges of the table leaf and top.

Shoulder: In a mortise-and-tenon joint, the part of the tenon perpendicular to the cheek. In a dovetail joint, the valleys between the pins or tails.

Sliding dovetail joint: A joinery method in which a dovetailed slide on one piece fits into a matching groove in the other.

Splay angle: The angle at which a chair leg or post deviates from the vertical when viewed from the front of the chair; see *rake angle*.

Steam bending: The technique of softening wood for bending by subjecting it to steam and heat, and then bending it around a curved form.

Stile: The vertical member of a frame-and-panel assembly; see *rail*.

Stopped dado: A dado that stops before crossing the full width or thickness of a workpiece.

Substrate: A piece of plywood or solid wood used as the foundation for veneer or leather that covers the surface of a desk top.

Template: A pattern cut from plywood, hardwood, or particleboard used to produce multiple copies of a part.

Tenon: A protrusion from the end of a board that fits into a mortise.

Tester: A light framework that joins the tops of the bedposts in a four-poster bed, often used to hang a canopy or drapery.

Through dovetail joint: A method of joining wood at the corners by means of interlocking pins and tails, both cut through the thickness of the workpiece.

Travisher: A type of spokeshave designed for smoothing concave surfaces.

Urn: A decorative element turned in spindle work; often part of a finial.

Veneer: A thin layer of decorative wood used to dress up a more common species of wood.

Wood button: A small, square-shaped block with a rabbet at one end that is used to secure the top of a piece of furniture.

Wood movement: The shrinking or swelling of wood in reaction to changes in relative humidity.

INDEX

ACKNOWLEDGMENTS

The editors wish to thank the following:

CLASSIC AMERICAN FURNITURE STYLES
Winterthur Museum, Winterthur, DE

PEMBROKE TABLE
Adjustable Clamp Co., Chicago, IL; Albert Constantine and Son Inc., Bronx, NY; American Tool Cos., Lincoln, NE; Black & Decker/Elu Power Tools, Towson, MD; CMT Tools, Oldsmar, FL; Delta International Machinery/Porter-Cable, Guelph, Ont.; Great Neck Saw Mfrs. Inc. (Buck Bros. Division), Millbury, MA; Les Realisations Loeven-Morcel, Montreal, Que.; Sears, Roebuck and Co., Chicago, IL; Stanley Tools, Division of the Stanley Works, New Britain, CT; Tool Trend Ltd., Concord, Ont.; Vacuum Pressing Systems Inc., Brunswick, ME; Wainbee Ltd., Pointe Claire, Que./DE-STA-CO, Troy, MI; The Woodworker's Store, Rogers, MN

FOUR-POSTER BED
Adjustable Clamp Co., Chicago, IL; American Tool Cos., Lincoln, NE; CMT Tools, Oldsmar, FL; Delta International Machinery/Porter-Cable, Guelph, Ont.; Great Neck Saw Mfrs. Inc. (Buck Bros. Division), Millbury, MA; Jean-Pierre Masse, Montreal, Que.; Packard Woodworks, Tryon, NC; Record Tools, Inc., Pickering, Ont.; Ryobi America Corp., Anderson, SC; Sears, Roebuck and Co., Chicago, IL; Stanley Tools, Division of the Stanley Works, New Britain, CT; Woodcraft Supply Corp., Parkersburg, WV

WINDSOR CHAIR
Adjustable Clamp Co., Chicago, IL; Anglo-American Enterprises Corp., Somerdale, NJ; Mike Dunbar, Portsmouth, NH; Great Neck Saw Mfrs. Inc. (Buck Bros. Division), Millbury, MA; Drew Langsner, Marshall, NC; Lee Valley Tools, Ltd., Ottawa, Ont.; Olde Mill Cabinet Shoppe, York, PA; Stanley Tools, Division of the Stanley Works, New Britain, CT

QUEEN ANNE SECRETARY
Adjustable Clamp Co., Chicago, IL; Albert Constantine and Son Inc., Bronx, NY; American Tool Cos., Lincoln, NE; CMT Tools, Oldsmar, FL; Delta International Machinery/Porter-Cable, Guelph, Ont.; Great Neck Saw Mfrs. Inc. (Buck Bros. Division), Millbury, MA; David Keller, Petaluma, CA; Lee Valley Tools, Ltd. Ottawa, Ont.; Les Realisations Loeven-Morcel, Montreal, Que.; Sears, Roebuck and Co., Chicago, IL; Steiner-Lamello A.G. Switzerland/Colonial Saw Co., Kingston, MA; Tool Trend Ltd., Concord, Ont.; Vacuum Pressing Systems Inc., Brunswick, ME; Wainbee Ltd., Pointe Claire, Que./DE-STA-CO, Troy, MI

The following persons also assisted in the preparation of this book:

Lorraine Doré, Sylvie Girard, Solange Laberge, Geneviève Monette, David Simon.

PICTURE CREDITS

Cover Robert Chartier
6,7 Ron Levine
8,9 Tom Wolff
10,11 Robert Holmes
14,16 Courtesy of The Henry Francis du Pont Wintherthur Museum
18 Martin Fox